*Marvin Rosen, PhD*

**W9-BRR-224**

# Treating Children in Out-of-Home Placements

*Pre-publication*
*REVIEW*

"For the college and graduate student and/or the professional working in the social services arena, Dr. Rosen successfully presents through written dialogue, experience, and research the merits of placement outside the family structure. Of special interest is Rosen's attention to the presentation of many of the precursors of challenging behaviors as well as the significant and critical 'agents of change' (e.g., the effectiveness of well-trained direct care staff) necessary in any supportive residential or foster care program. Two conceptual models of therapeutic intervention along with selected treatment supports necessary for a successful therapeutic milieu are presented."

**David H. Rice, PhD**
*Vice President,*
*Behavioral Health Services,*
*Woods Services, Inc.,*
*Langhorne, PA*

# Treating Children
# in Out-of-Home Placements

# THE HAWORTH PRESS
New, Recent, and Forthcoming Titles
of Related Interest

*Treating Children with Sexually Abusive Behavior Problems: Guidelines for Child and Parent Intervention* by Jan Ellen Burton and Lucinda A. Rasmussen

*Sibling Abuse Trauma: Assessment and Intervention Strategies for Children, Families, and Adults* by John V. Caffaro and Allison Conn-Caffaro

*The Learning About Myself (LAMS) Program for At-Risk Parents: Learning from the Past—Changing the Future* by Verna Rickard

*The Learning About Myself (LAMS) Program for At-Risk Parents: Handbook for Group Participants* by Verna Rickard

*Bridging Worlds: Understanding and Facilitating Adolescent Recovery from the Trauma of Abuse* by Joycee Kennedy and Carol McCarthy

*Cedar House: A Model Child Abuse Treatment Program* by Bobbi Kendig with Clara Lowry

*Multiple Victimization of Children: Conceptual, Developmental, Research, and Treatment Issues* edited by B. B. Robbie Rossman and Mindy S. Rosenberg

*Sexual, Physical, and Emotional Abuse in Out-of-Home Care: Prevention Skills for At-Risk Children* by Toni Cavanagh Johnson

# Treating Children in Out-of-Home Placements

Marvin Rosen, PhD

The Haworth Press
New York • London

The Haworth Press, Inc., 10 Alice Street, Binghamton, NY 13904-1580

Soft cover edition published 1999.

Cover design by Monica L. Seifert.

**The Library of Congress has cataloged the hardcover edition of this book as:**

Rosen, Marvin.
    Treating children in out-of-home placements / Marvin Rosen.
        p.   cm.
    Includes bibliographical references and index.
    ISBN 0-7890-0163-2 (alk. paper).
    1. Abused children—Care—United States. 2. Abused children—Services for—United States. 3. Abused children—Mental health—United States. 4. Adopted children—Mental health—United States. 5. Foster home care—United States. 6. Child mental health services—United States. I. Title.
HV6626.52.R67 1998
362.76′8′0973—DC21
                                                      97-45116
                                                       CIP

ISBN: 0–7890–0893–9 (pbk.)

To Joyce, my lifemate, who wants me to write poetry.
To Abe, old roommate, friend, and colleague, who suggested
the connective tissue.
To the children of Cottage Four and Cottage Six.

## ABOUT THE AUTHOR

**Marvin Rosen, PhD,** is a psychologist at Elwyn Institutes in Elwyn, Pennsylvania. Dr. Rosen has interned at the Veteran's Administration Hospital in Perry Point, Maryland, and worked as a Clinical Psychologist at Albert Einstein Medical Center in Philadelphia. Dr. Rosen began working for Elwyn Institutes in 1963, serving first as Director of Psychology and then Clinical Director, Assistant to the President, Vice President for Development, and Vice President for Research, implementing Elwyn Institutes' Preschool Language Acquisition and directing its Head Trauma Program. He also acted as Principal Investigator for a follow-up investigation involving mentally retarded persons and community living, which resulted in numerous publications and a textbook, *Habilitations of the Handicapped* (with Gerald R. Clark, MD, and Marvin S. Kivitz, PhD). Dr. Rosen has written or edited six textbooks on mental retardation, psychology, and rehabilitation. He has been a consultant to the Devereaux Foundation since 1988. Most recently, he has provided family counseling and training services in Elwyn's Children's Division and helped develop a Residential Treatment Facility, while maintaining his private practice in Media, Pennsylvania.

# CONTENTS

# Foreword

After a brief but incisive panoramic view of the history of foster homes and treatment care, Dr. Rosen begins his in-depth exploration of front-line staff working with troubled children. By carefully assessing research in the field he is able to cite practical characteristics and strategies that are most beneficial for emotionally disturbed children.

Dr. Rosen presents a critical but balanced review of diagnostic systems now used in the field. In a nonjargon style, he reviews both their strengths and disadvantages, especially the danger of negative stereotyping.

In Chapter 5 Dr. Rosen presents specific guidelines for working with abused and disadvantaged children that can be useful for parents and all parental surrogates within or outside of residential care.

Throughout his study Dr. Rosen is careful to cite the pertinent research that confirms his analysis and conclusions of the nature of children's problems and treatment programs that work.

In concise elegant terms Dr. Rosen summarizes major contemporary approaches to treatment—psychodynamic, cognitive-behavioral, and family systems (Chapter 7) and he deconstructs the good and bad features in each of them. Dr. Rosen avoids the pitfall of having to choose one orientation and is able to use helpful interventions from all the approaches.

Dr. Rosen emphasizes the importance of teaching and modeling sound values (Chapter 9) in a joint effort by therapists and direct care staff. He carefully reviews the use of medication and cites pertinent research to back up his recommendations (Chapter 11).

Dr. Rosen emphasizes throughout his study that "each child carries with him or her a basic will to preserve their own integrity" (Chapter 12). This basic principle thoroughly informs all of Dr.

Rosen's work. It is an excellent beginning principle and also a magnificent one to end this review of a very enlightening up-to-date, well-researched study!

*Howard W. Polsky, PhD*
*Professor of Social Science*
*and Research,*
*Columbia University*
*School of Social Work*

# Preface

Two friends met for dinner at a gourmet restaurant. Both in their sixties, they were renewing a forty-year-old relationship. Together they began their careers as psychologists as roommates and classmates at the university. The first became a social and industrial psychologist and found success in the business world. Always a risk taker, at age sixty-one he had started flying lessons. The second, a clinical psychologist, had worked most of his professional life for the same nonprofit, human service organization. He found some success in writing but never attained the highest pinnacles of professional development from either clinical practice or writing.

The dinner was a means of reminiscing, mutual unburdening, seeking counsel, and maintaining a relationship that both accepted as precious to them, transcending time and circumstance. The conversation turned to the work of the second. Coming back from a two-year respite from the nonprofit organization, when he went back briefly to teaching and private practice, his work was now related to a new commitment of the organization to provide residential treatment for emotionally disturbed adolescents. His friend, interested in the concept, probed in his own Socratic manner, exploring both the practicality of the venture as well as its clinical intricacies. The conversation became animated as the first drew out the second, challenging, seeking further elaboration, and sometimes adding insights of his own. The dialogue touched on major issues of care and treatment, costs, administration, outcomes, hurdles, and the like. The evening passed rapidly but demanded some closure.

"It's an interesting challenge," the first offered. "Why don't you write it up?"

"I'd have to find some way of combining academic-style review articles with practical issues."

"How would you tie that all together?"

"I don't know."

"I have an idea . . . Why don't you have two friends talking? The clinician could describe the program to his friend who would ask meaningful questions, drawing the other out. It might work . . . "

\* \* \*

America's treatment of at-risk children is receiving increasing attention in the media as well as national conferences, workshops, task forces, and the professional literature. Solutions are offered, successful programs are reported, and the sensitivities of educators, child welfare workers, clinicians, and the general public are aroused. Yet, the problem continues. Today's solutions become tomorrow's failures. Thousands of cast-off children, products of society's most serious problems, are referred each year for residential care, foster home placement, psychiatric treatment, or juvenile detention. Some of these children somehow survive and succeed in becoming responsible and productive adults. Others will remain on the fringe of an affluent society, trapped within the bonds of drugs, poverty, unemployment, and a welfare system designed to help them but instead perpetuating itself from one generation to the next.

This book does not attempt to solve the pressing issues that create dependent and emotionally disturbed children. Nor does it offer compelling solutions to their care and treatment. Less ambitious in scope, it outlines critical issues and concepts. This book attempts to honestly depict the challenges inherent in trying to develop and administer a treatment program for seriously disturbed children.

The adolescents who find their way to residential treatment facilities (RTFs) represent problems that are national in scope—poverty, drugs, and dysfunctional families. Many are streetwise kids from the inner city. Others are from suburban areas but no less damaged. Still others come from rural areas. Most are the results of broken or dysfunctional families. Many have suffered physical or sexual abuse. All have psychiatric diagnoses. Some appear immediately to be victims; they are vulnerable, passive, and easily led by the more aggressive peers. Most, however, are tough, belligerent, "in your face" kids who will not be denied. Destructive, rebellious, and suspicious of adults, clever in seizing attention and challenging those trying hard to help them, they manage to disrupt the most structured program. No amount of nurturing, even spoiling, seems sufficient to soothe their hurts, win them over, or make them buy into the middle-class values of those now responsible for their welfare. Yet, some do manage to make remarkable gains without relinquishing their own self-defined integrity as hardened, emotionally impervious, tough guys. Staff learn to view them, not as juvenile delinquents, although such labels might apply, but as survivors trying to protect themselves against a society that has failed them. We learn not to challenge their basic identities, yet somehow we seduce them into a reasonable facsimile of cooperation.

What follows is a review of the treatment of children in placement in this country, the issues involved, and the ways these concerns have been addressed. We will argue in this book that the children treated in RTFs deserve competent professional treatment and that they may not always receive it. We will support the development of unifying, conceptual models in RTFs that extend beyond regulations and principles of care promulgated by consumer advocacy organizations. Furthermore, the models developed should not be the same across all treatment centers. A variety of approaches to treatment have evolved over the years, but there is little basis to choose one over the other. Unless residential treatment centers adopt unifying, consistent treatment approaches, outcome studies, which are rarely performed anyway, will be of little value. If one RTF works better than another, there will be no understanding of the reasons determining the superiority. It will become apparent in this book that, although the problem of children requiring out-of-home placements has been with us since colonial times, we have really made very little progress in solving this problem. Foster care has not fulfilled its promise of family reunification. Residential treatment facilities may be less effective than their precursors and less likely to produce "permanency" arrangements for the child.

This book consists of a number of review chapters in areas that are intimately related to the treatment issues. They are regarded by the author as a basic framework for understanding the needs of the children and the efforts in this country to meet those needs. Chapter 1 is a review of the history of attempts to deal with a child welfare population of children in out-of-home placements in this country. Many children were "placed in" large orphanages, precursors of today's RTFs. Chapter 2 reviews the practice of the "placing out" of children in foster homes. In Chapter 3, the current diagnostic system for emotional disorders is briefly described. Chapter 4 details the evolution of one current diagnosis relevant to RTFs. Conduct disorder and other behavioral diagnoses trace their origins to early concepts of the "moral imbecile." The staffing of RTFs is addressed in Chapter 5. The roots of the major types of problems of children in placement arise from histories of violence and abuse and disturbances in the basic processes of attachment. Literature discussing the impact of these conditions is reviewed in Chapter 6. Chapters 7 through 11 cover the major efforts of intervention that attempt to remediate emotional disturbance, including psychotherapy, family counseling, and the use of medication. Chapter 9 argues that one aspect of teaching—the teaching of values—is often ignored in present-day treatment programs.

This book concludes by discussing two treatment models that appear to be applicable to children in placement. The first is a cognitive therapy approach based upon assumptions of the cognitive makeup of children who have the backgrounds described previously. The second is a developmental model that addresses self-esteem, attachment and belonging, mastery, autonomy, and values. The dialogues that precede each chapter were included to convey the message that this book is more than a collection of review chapters. The conversations depicted represent more than two people talking. Rather, they convey that the RTF which provided the impetus for this book was a living entity with real people planning, implementing, arguing, and obsessing over issues that underlie the programs—issues that have not been fully resolved at centers serving similar populations.

*   *   *

"Hey, white boy. You own this building?"

The challenge made by Randy, as I entered Pierson Hall for a meeting, was not atypical, and I responded without rancor. Randy, age sixteen and African American, is a referral from out of state. An aggressive and constantly provocative child, he has been involved in numerous fights and destructive acts since being enrolled at a sixteen-bed, residential dormitory that focuses on the management of difficult behaviors. I have spent over thirty years in various clinical, research, and administrative capacities, but none of it prepared me for the kinds of kids we were now accepting.

*Marvin Rosen*

# Chapter 1

# Child Saving in America

"You need to understand something about the children."

"Juvenile delinquents."

"No, we don't accept those that have been adjudicated delinquent."

"You're splitting hairs. You've told me what they do. Your kids just haven't been caught yet."

"They come from terrible backgrounds—abuse, neglect, abandonment. You're a social psychologist; you know what poverty can do."

"And you used to be a hard-nosed empiricist. You've become a bleeding heart."

"I haven't forgotten my empirical roots. Granted, we've not done what we should in studying the effectiveness of the treatment or the program. We're working on it. We do measure progress toward preestablished goals, but that's not the point here. I don't need data to know that these kids have been hurt by society. I don't know much about child welfare. I guess it started with orphanages. It wasn't part of what we were taught in graduate school."

"There's a whole lot we weren't taught. Our curriculum was primarily experimental psychology. I can still trace the history of our field from Helmholtz's physiological foundations, through the structuralism of Wundt and Titchner, the behaviorism of Pavlov, Watson, and Skinner, to present-day cognitive psychology. But child welfare and children in placement were new to me."

"I guess our mentors didn't find it important—too practical, too applied. You want to know about orphans and delinquents, go read about it yourself. We stay purely scientific here at Penn. So how did it all begin?"

\* \* \*

Wollons (1993) traces the changes in dealing with dependent and delinquent children in the United States from "an intense colonial religious need for salvation, with the church in authority, to the nineteenth-century need for order and citizenship, controlled by private philanthropy in local communities, to the twentieth-century belief in individual development with law, science, and government as arbiters" (Wollons, 1993, p. iv).

During the seventeenth century, children were the sole responsibility of their parents, with the father having absolute authority, although the social and religious goals of child rearing derived from the church. Disobedient children were typically placed as apprentices. Orphaned children became members of expanded or stepfamilies. The greatest risks to children were childbirth and disease.

By the mid-eighteenth century, a variety of public charitable institutions began to replace the family in providing for children in need. Almshouses cared for the poor, the widowed, the orphaned, and the mentally ill. Public social policy became permeated with new ideas about individualism and secularism. Rising educational standards prolonged economic dependency. Goals for children expanded from salvation and religious life to education and health. By the end of the century, methods of adoption were developed through the Orphans' Court.

The nineteenth century brought a rapid increase in the population of cities and large numbers of foreign immigrants. The Civil War swelled the numbers of orphans, and there were new classes of black and female juvenile delinquents overcrowding the reformatories that developed to house them. Nineteenth-century reformers blamed juvenile crime on poverty, heredity, immigration, and urbanization. Social Darwinists and hereditarians pointed fingers at groups of children born of "inferior stock." Most orphanages were privately supported. The Children's Aid Society of New York City, for example, became a model of private welfare organizations, placing thousands of orphans in foster-care lodging houses of industrial schools. Custody laws began to favor mothers. The school became a significant force for instilling social values and control over the lives of children. Children's deviant behavior began to be attributed as much to environmental factors as to personal flaws. Moralistic conceptions gave way to an appreciation of sociocultural, economic, and psychological factors.

Cravens (1993) identifies two distinct eras in "child saving": concern and legislation. From the 1870s to the 1920s, concern was focused on abnormal or deviant groups, such as children with delinquent behaviors or mental retardation. This was the era of the growth of institutions and the development of the juvenile court system. The era from 1920 to 1950 was characterized by a greater concern for the normal child, with teaching geared toward adaptation to societal norms.

Public school systems beginning with kindergarten were perceived as a mechanism for molding minds, teaching morality, and inculcating proper health habits. Compulsory education had been enacted in most states by 1900, and federal child labor legislation began in 1916. Particular concern was expressed about children from immigrant and poor families who must learn to become responsible citizens. School programs were designed to include hygiene and health care, athletics and physical education, achievement testing, and guidance counseling. Child saving was passed to experts—scientists and therapists seen as having the competence to handle complex social problems. Interrupted briefly by the Great Depression, the child-saving movement gained new impetus during the New Deal era of Franklin Roosevelt. Children benefited indirectly from the economic recovery and greater availability of jobs for adults that arose under the new social welfare programs. Social Security legislation, aid to dependent children, and mothers' pensions all had impact upon children at risk.

By the 1950s, there was another broad trend affecting children, with greater emphasis on the individual rather than the group. The dogma of individuation was spurred on by the "me-ism of the 1970s and 1980s. Public concern for the poor, the stigmatized, and the oppressed during the Roosevelt era gave way to the entitlement philosophy of the 1980s and 1990s. The rights of all children as individuals were emphasized. Individual child development was focused on by psychologists, as opposed to earlier cross-sectional studies of large groups. The civil rights movement heralded demands by all groups for their full benefits as citizens. The rebellion of youth against social conformity is seen by some as gaining expression for the first time at Woodstock. The optimism of the Kennedy and Johnson years spawned an attitude that all social problems could be solved by proper technology and environmental improvement. Headstart, deinstitutionalization, and the mainstreaming of handicapped children were some of the most important repercussions. Recognition of the rights of children reached its zenith. But these good intentions also highlighted the continuing plight of the most disadvantaged children—those of African-American heritage, those living in urban slums, those with severe emotional problems, and those who were the victims of physical, sexual, and emotional abuse. These children, many well known to the social welfare and the criminal justice systems, continued to present insurmountable problems that no degree of enlightenment, sensitivity, or modern technology could successfully address.

It is only relatively recently in the history of our country that communities, states, and the federal government assumed responsibility for problem children, or children in general. Throughout America's early years, such functions as the care of children were relegated to the family or the Church. It is only since the mid-nineteenth century that governments established organized programs for the care of children who are considered vulnerable—the destitute, delinquent, and mentally and socially disadvantaged. This change in perceived public responsibility brought about the regulation of child labor, public education, improved health care, and laws regarding the use of tobacco, alcohol, and pornography. From this time, we observe increasing concern about children placed at risk from poverty, disease, unwholesome living conditions, poor education, abuse, discrimination, and crime.

One of the most successful solutions to the plight of poor, homeless children was a movement in New York City that began in the 1850s. At that time, as many as 30,000 homeless children wandered the streets of the city, living under the most pitiful conditions. Labeled "street arabs" by the police, they were regarded as a "dangerous class," threatening society. Many were the children of immigrants to this country who came seeking cheap land and a new life in rural America but instead wound up in the slums of our large cities. "They existed by any means at hand, by begging, picking pockets, snatching purses, and by shoplifting. Some ran errands for gambling operations. Some were forced into prostitution. Their lives were generally a steady progression from petty offenses to serious crime to imprisonment . . . " (Patrick, Sheets, and Trickel, 1990, pp. 21-22).

In 1853, the Reverend Charles Loring Brace and a few other reformers founded the Children's Aid Society in New York City. Going beyond merely providing food and shelter in orphan asylums, the Society attempted to provide education and vocational training.

Brace's solution to the problem of abandoned children was the "placing out" of children on farms in rural areas of the West and South. Such children were to be made part of the family (rather than indentured) and provided with all the rights and responsibilities of the couple's natural children. Local committees of respectable citizens from the communities were organized to screen foster parents in advance. The first trainload of children left New York City in September, 1954, to Dowagiac, Michigan. This was the first of many "orphan trains" that served to relocate thousands of children until well into this century. Although the effort was criticized by some as sending the children into slavery and by others as inflicting criminals upon our nation's farmers, many of the children did adjust to their new homes and led useful, happy, and productive lives.

## ORPHANAGES

David Vanbiema, in a *Time* magazine article (December 12, 1994) asked, "Have America's attempts to find families for its abandoned and damaged children failed so badly that some institutionalization looks good?" (p. 59). The article, instigated by recent remarks by the present Speaker of the House about orphanages for children of poor, unwed, teenage mothers, points out that, although federal law mandates family-based care over institutions, many families have proven themselves incapable of parenting, and foster care has all too often proven itself "an equally cruel form of neglect and abuse by the state." In such cases, institutional care within residential treatment centers (today's equivalent of orphanages) may be instrumental in providing a sense of permanency that revolving-door foster placements have failed to accomplish. Although most residential treatment centers have not flown in the face of deinstitutionalization and family preservation concepts, by returning children to their families or foster families after short residential placements, others have maintained children for years, and some have advocated the need for children to grow up within the institution.

What, then, were orphanages? Were they the Dickensian depiction of abuse and neglect with which we are familiar? Can only a Daddy Warbucks rescue Li'l Orphan Annie? One account (Reeder, 1909) provides quite a different picture.

Reeder was superintendent of the New York Orphan Asylum, Hastings-on-Hudson, New York. The book reads as a guide to parents in bringing up their children. Liberally peppered with photographs depicting the children at school, work, and play, the book might well have represented much of the philosophy at many such facilities. The children had recently been moved from a single-structure city facility, and much of the author's criticism seems to be directed at the earlier program. The need for a well-balanced and varied diet with children in the cottages participating in the meal preparation is stressed. "Ice cream sodas, . . . gingerbread, and other appetite incentives may be used in a very effective and wholesome manner when properly correlated with other interests and activities necessary to the development of the child. In fact, a child's life is barren without them . . . " (Reeder, 1909, p. 35). Proper exercise and play in natural environments are also extolled as a necessary ingredient, especially in children coming from slum tenements with little freedom of movement.

In addition to a wholesome environment, good health, and a public school education, the child's need for learning self-reliance and initiative are addressed through industrial training. Rather than employ them in dull, factory-type labor, the author advocates allowing the children to use their own initiative in preparing a meal, raising children, growing tomato plants, and marketing their products. "These boys and girls—janitors, storekeepers, gardeners, house cleaners, cooks, etc.—are working and going to school. They are laying the foundation for independent self-support at an early age. They are held strictly responsible for the work assigned to them, and are fined for, or required to make good, losses resulting from wastefulness, carelessness or neglect" (Reeder, 1909, p. 82). In this way, a sense of responsibility was developed. Girls learned to mend and darn, clean and take care of a house, cook, serve in the dining room, cultivate flowers and vegetables, and care for the younger children. Boys learned to use tools, make useful articles around the home, chop wood, use a hoe and shovel, drive and care for horses, and raise poultry.

Reeder also emphasized the importance of giving boys and girls some comprehension of the relation between work and wages. The lack of such economic training, he maintained, resulted in exploitation by employers. He provided as evidence of this the stories of several children "placed out" at farms in the west, working for years as "white slaves" for farmers for only their room and board. At age twenty-one and after working seven or eight years doing the work of an adult, they were often put out by the farmer with little more than the clothes on their back.

> The only practical training which will prepare boys and girls to look out for themselves after they leave their orphanage home is a work and wage experience while there. In this Home, we are paying over eight hundred dollars a year to the children of the Orphanage for work that they do as cooks, laundresses, seamstresses, gardeners, janitors . . . There is no charity in this. We do not pay for work which we would not otherwise be obliged to hire done, nor do we pay more than it is worth . . . The economic training given the boys and girls . . . involves four factors: how to earn money, how to save money, how to spend money, and how to give money. (pp. 105-106)

The children had savings accounts at community banks and were obliged to buy their own clothing, toilet articles, and other possessions from their earnings. Each child was obliged to keep an itemized expense account that would be inspected each month. Reeder acknowledged that many institutional homes were not being run to such standards.

After extolling the virtues of public school education, Reeder endorsed the use of an institutional-based school for his children. By integrating industrial training, practical experience, and academics the program becomes more relevant to the lives of the children and more motivating. Lessons are drawn from the everyday experience of the child rather than from the abstract book learning more typical in regular schools. He believed that this approach would better prepare the child to be able to support him or herself at the age of fifteen or sixteen. Discipline was imposed by means of fines and deprivation of privileges. Corporal punishment was disapproved of, although not legislated away since the child needs to learn the reality of authority. Reeder believed that children kept busy with ample opportunity to earn money for productive work were far less likely to create mischief.

Indeed, moral training was considered to be a backbone of the program. Lamenting that moral and religious instruction were no longer included within the curricula of public schools, Reeder attributed the increase in the frequency of juvenile delinquency to dissolution of family values, the rise in the population of cities, and the increase in immigration. Moral training at the orphanage was viewed as more than merely informing the child about moral standards and ideals. Rather, it meant also the freedom to choose right from wrong and the provision of moral experiences and object lessons. Children were often guided to impose their own disciplinary actions upon an errant member, although they were not given absolute authority for fear of abuse. Excellence in work or conduct was rewarded, responsibility and trust were invested in the child, and punishments were chosen to fit the crime. Reeder saw the orphanage as responsible for teaching societal values regarding personal habits, purity, temperance, and righteous living.

## FAMILIES

The treatment of families is recent in the broad range of mental health services. This approach probably originated in the child guidance clinics that were funded nationally in the 1920s, modeled after Chicago's Juvenile Psychopathic Institute and the Judge Baker Clinic in Boston. These clinics were established to provide psychological treatment to children and to their parents, although the orientation, reflecting the behaviorism of the day, was largely "habit training." Those children whose behavior was regarded as too difficult to manage in a family setting were provided custodial care in large, public mental hospitals or congregate care facilities in the child welfare or juvenile justice system.

By the early 1970s, as a result of the new emphasis on advocacy and human rights, deinstitutionalization and normalization was applied to juvenile populations and families were now being expected to solve many of the problems previously relegated to large, congregate, residential living centers. Public Law 99-457, which mandates early identification and treatment of special needs children, focuses upon families, rather than children, as the targets of service delivery. The Child and Adolescent Service System Program (CASSP)* (1984) provided the impetus for family-based services to children within the mental health system and encouraged the collaboration of community agencies and systems in service delivery. Unlike family therapy models that treat the parents as a pathological source of the child's problems, the new emphasis on family treatment is geared toward improving the resources, internal and external, available to families for coping with family problems.

Research into the factors operative in the family system with children has yielded one consistent finding. Children who demonstrate resilience to the environmental stresses typically identified with their problems share a common characteristic—the existence of a supportive family member who provided consistent nurturance and who became an active participant in the interventions applied to the child. This degree of support appears to provide the ingredient needed to withstand the stresses determining emotional disturbance in high-risk children. Even children who have lived in adverse environments, including violence and drug-related activities, had favorable outcomes, provided they could rely upon a nurturant and supportive caregiver. Goodman and Brumley (1990), for example, found that responsiveness of mothers and their affectional involvement with their children was predictive of the children's favorable social/emotional functioning over time.

---

*The CASSP program is supported by federal legislation guided by a system of care concept developed by Stroul and Friedman (1986) addressing the needs of emotionally disturbed children and adolescents. The system of care perspective focuses on broadening and strengthening the community base as the essential arena for treatment and rehabilitation.

## RESIDENTIAL PROGRAMS

In 1962, a young sociologist at Columbia named Howard Polsky published a small volume (Polsky, 1962) analyzing the social structure at Hollymeade, a residential treatment unit for delinquent youth outside New York City. Using a participant observer method with the cottage housing the toughest boys at the facility, Polsky applied social work theory and techniques in investigating the unit as a tightly organized social structure. Because of the similarity between the first Cottage Six and our own work, it is necessary to devote some space to the earlier effort and to point out some important differences.

Polsky made some important assumptions in designing his research—assumptions that led him in directions consistent with his basic premise, i.e., that the social system in which the individual is embedded is a potent force in determining the behavior of the individual. Leonard Cottrell, who wrote the foreword to Polsky's book, summarized this premise as follows:

> The social system in Cottage Six appeared not only to be the dominant force in the life of the boys living there but was potent enough to evoke a kind of covert and unwitting support and collaboration from the institution itself. Moreover, the removal of "key" boys did not appear to affect the viability of the cultural patterns in the least. Other boys simply moved into or were put into the vacated roles. (1962, p. 7)

Indeed, Polsky appeared to attribute minor significance to the psychoanalytically oriented treatment program, overseen by psychiatrists and imposed by psychiatric caseworkers, cottage parents, and school supervisors. Instead, the primary cottage social group, in this case forming a "deviant subculture," appeared to Polsky to be the most powerful determinant of individual behaviors in Cottage Six: "Hollymeade's circumscribed setting thus affords us an unusual stage on which to spotlight a deviant peer group and how it defines various roles for its members" (1962, p. 20).

Hollymeade housed dependent children supported by the Department of Welfare, private agencies, and the courts. Although the facility served children between the ages of twelve and eighteen,

Cottage Six was a senior cottage in which about twenty older adolescents resided. Those residents who could not adjust to the subculture in the cottage were discharged.

Polsky outlined the means by which the cottage group regulated the behavior of its members. Mechanisms of aggression, deviant activities, threats, "ranking," and scapegoating played an important part in structuring the relationships among the group members and the social positions they occupied within the group. The dominant pattern of aggression permeated and defined the group. Power, exerted through intimidation and physical domination, was the principal means by which members structured themselves into high- and low-status positions. Physical strength and aggressiveness were valued traits and formed the basis of ultimate authority among the boys. Program staff tacitly accepted the roles of individual group members and generally did not intervene in their relationships with each other. Aggression was expressed both externally to members of other cottages as well as internally among the group members.

Deviant activities such as gambling were also an integral part of the group culture. Verbal threats, shaming, harassment, insulting (ranking), and scapegoating of weaker, lower status members was constant. Subgroups or cliques were rigidly maintained and formalized by labels such as "big man," con-artist, punk, queer, and bush boy, and they determined all facets of cottage life, such as seating designations in the dining hall. Movement in status occurred when higher status members left the group or when power was successfully challenged through physical confrontations. This deviant culture was passed on to new boys as they entered the program so that old roles were maintained by newer members. The group had a history that was perpetuated. Rather than viewing this deviancy as pathological or dysfunctional, Polsky described the behaviors as "a crucial component in the equilibrium of cottage social organization" (1962, p. 85). Cottage parents reinforced the delinquent subculture by maintaining loyalty to the group, supporting the social hierarchy, wooing the leaders, and physically dominating the weaker members. "A *quid pro quo* relationship prevailed" (p. 134).

Cottage parents were dissociated from the professional (psychoanalytic) philosophy of the treatment team. Polsky saw little likelihood that the values of the treatment staff would influence the cottage subculture. Staff represented middle-class values of individualism, achievement, and upward mobility. The boys, on the other hand, were from a culture that emphasized authoritarian, defeatist roles and mastery of the world through aggressive intimidation. Staff were predisposed to interpret cottage behavior as deviant, pathological, infantile, and provocative rather than as a functional accommodation to an already aggressive environment. Therapists, who saw the children in their offices, had little chance of changing the pressures the group placed on the boys to "get along" by conforming to the expectations of the delinquent leaders of the group. "The professional staff's values do not constitute a sufficiently strong countervailing force to overcome the negative values promoted by the cottage social system" (1962, p. 162).

As a psychologist, rather than social worker, the present author has a commitment toward understanding how individual personalities, unique histories, and family background determined behavior. The importance of the social group was not ignored but was seen as only another determining factor—one that played a major role in determining behavior within the institution but not necessarily at home. In fact, how the child behaves in placement is seen as less important than how he or she behaves on home visits and therapeutic leave. The purpose of the program is to return children home, preferably to their own families. Although the children behaved in a destructive manner on the institutional grounds and in their own residence building, this was expected, given their diagnoses and backgrounds. Destructive acts become the norm and are directly parallel to the deviant behaviors of Polsky's group.

There is a difference in this author's view of the children and their futures. As a therapist, I believe that many of them can overcome their backgrounds and will accept standards for behavior presented by staff and the therapeutic milieu. I believe that many of the children will see new options which were not available or visible to them in their dysfunctional families or inner-city neighborhoods. I believe that some will accept the desirability of change and their potential for change. This is explained in more detail in Chapters 7 and 8, which discuss therapeutic approaches.

Although Polsky provided a fascinating look at social process, he seemed to harbor no hope that the program would have permanent effects upon the boys. Rather, the primary, deviant subculture within the group would prevail, whether the boys stayed at Hollymeade or returned home. Indeed, his follow-up statistics confirmed his expectations. Many of the boys wound up in jail. Of twenty-six boys who were at Hollymeade when the study was performed, seventeen were later found to have made some degree of community adjustment, i.e., they were not in jail or AWOL from the army two years after discharge; they were mostly employed and maintaining themselves in the community. Of the nine labeled "deviant," four were in jails and five were in mental hospitals. (Two had been in jail and in a mental hospital.) Will our group fare better?

Polsky emphasized the dual cultures of staff and cottage life represented at Hollymeade that remained insulated from each other. Cottage houseparents clearly become part of the cottage subculture by accommodating the boys' aggressive and manipulative behaviors. The standards of professional staff were complementary to those of houseparents but far less powerful. Since the professional staff left by 5:00 p.m., the standards of the boys took over completely in their absence: "The professional staff who have the enthusiasm, understanding, and authority to aid the boys in becoming oriented to more positive values, fade from the picture with the setting sun" (1962, p. 137). The cottage staff, in turn, in an effort to maintain some degree of control, reinforced the deviant subculture so long as it did not disturb the very fabric of the cottage equilibrium. Behaviors that professional staff would regard as unacceptable were ignored or tolerated. Serious disruptions to cottage life, however, such as mass runaways, knifings, "rumbles," and liquor parties resulted in staff action, often with the assistance of the boys themselves. The deviant subculture persisted because it helped staff contain aggressive boys for limited time periods within the institutional setting.

Although staff in the present Cottage Six no doubt make similar accommodations to the children's aggressive and destructive behaviors, the dichotomy between professional and cottage values is less sharp. Treatment in our program is largely provided by the cottage staff who are based in the building. Although an outside clinical psychologist works with some of the children and their families, the Unit Director is herself a psychologist. She sees all of the children individually and supervises group counseling within the building. Counseling groups are reality-based, deriving not from psychoanalytic or other theoretical orientation but from the perceived needs of the children. All children participate in a sexuality group. There are also self-esteem groups, stress management groups, and groups that deal with depression, loneliness, and abandonment. The children accept these groups as part of their treatment. Group leaders are not professionally trained psychologists or social workers. What they lack in professional skills they make up for in their knowledge of the children and what is going on in the cottage.

Conclusions similar to those of Polsky were reached by Trieschman, Whittaker, and Brendtro (1969) and Trieschman (1976) in administering a program at the Walker School in Needham, Massachusetts. Again, therapists accustomed to providing outpatient therapy were hard pressed to deal with a twenty-four-hour residential program. "The child management skills necessary for one adult with one child in one office would not stretch to one adult and five children across the playground, into the shower and up to bed" (Trieschman, 1976, p. 124). The nature of residential treatment was defined as the other twenty-three hours outside of therapy that was critical to program success. Treatment was conceptualized, not as "curing illness" but as teaching "emotional competence"; i.e., teaching children skills of trusting, dealing with anger, sadness, and being alone, and togetherness. Insight and self-awareness, although important, did not help when one child was standing with a stick over the head of another, ready to strike. The importance of working within the community and with families, rather than in isolation in a treatment setting, was emphasized.

One novel approach to the treatment of juvenile offenders has been the use of boot camps run according to military norms for 90- or 120-day periods as an alternative to prison or detention centers (Polsky and Fast, 1993). The experience consists largely of rigorous physical training, march, and drill administered in a highly structured, sixteen-hour day. Close supervision of recreation, behavior, and personal life strictly enforces compliance with rules. Counseling, both during the program and in an after-care program, is also part of the regimen, with areas of leadership, self-esteem, and self-discipline being addressed. The atmosphere is one of direct confrontation by staff, physical punishment, often as a group, and intimidation by tough staff. Federally funded pilot programs have been run in Denver, Mobile, and Cleveland. Although the shock treatment style of haranguing is successful in producing obedience to authority during the boot-camp experience, recidivism is no different from that found after more traditional juvenile detention programs. Polsky and Fast suggest that the boot-camp experience is not enough and should be followed by training in life skills, problem solving, self-realization, and vocational competence.

Another program that began as a type of orphanage and continues today is Boys Town, in Omaha, Nebraska. Popularized in the movie starring Mickey Rooney and Spencer Tracy, the original program was established for homeless orphans. The philosophy expounded by its founder, Father Flanagan, is still endorsed by the present program (Jendryka, 1991). From the days of Father Flanagan, Boys Town's credo has been: "There's no such thing as a bad boy—only bad environment, bad thinking, and bad training." The original program was a highly structured setting with a strong religious component (boys learned to pray but were not told how to pray). According to school authorities, children learned to stay out of trouble.

In recent times, Boys Town radically changed its profile. Large, spartan dormitories were replaced with seventy-six single-family homes, each housing eight children. A family model was adopted with a married couple called "family teachers" living in each unit and serving as unit directors around the clock. Behavior modification was imposed as a skills-training regimen and a point system through which the children earned both necessities and privileges. The children are referred from other residential treatment programs, shelters, psychiatric hospitals, or foster homes. They carry emotional scars of physical and sexual abuse, and many have criminal backgrounds. Among the skills taught by the Boys Town program are how to get and hold a job, engage in relationships, follow instructions, accept criticism, accept "no" for an answer, greet someone, get the teacher's attention, make a request, and disagree appropriately.

A recent volume by Brendtro, Brokenleg, and Van Bockern (1990) presents a holistic Native American philosophy of child development and applies it to the task of reclaiming children at risk. Four characteristics of troubled children are addressed: destructive relationships stemming from a need for love but an inability to trust; feelings of futility, powerlessness, inadequacy, and fear of failure; learned habits of irresponsibility resulting in indifference, defiance, and rebellious behavior; and loss of purpose and self-centeredness.

Brendtro, Brokenleg, and Van Bockern are critical of the value placed upon obedience in American schools, a system of control that is foreign to Native American cultures and one that promotes coercion rather than caring and cooperation. In structuring a "reclaiming" environment, four factors are stressed: first is a feeling of belonging to a supportive community. Nurturance should be solely the role of biological parents but should include the child's acceptance and support of a larger circle of significant others. Kinship in tribal settings extends beyond biological relationships and teaches children that all people are interdependent. Second is the importance of mastery over one's environment. The child has a need to be competent, which, once satisfied, enhances motivation for further achievement. Third is the need to learn independence, i.e., involving youth in determining their own future while recognizing society's need to control harmful behavior. Children need to learn a sense of power and autonomy. Children must learn to respond to self-imposed controls rather than to the demands of others. At the same time, children learn to respect elders. Children are given reasons for their behavior rather than forced to submit to blind rules. Children should be provided increasing opportunities to make choices. Finally, children must learn to become caregivers rather than merely helpless recipients of the care of adults. Generosity and altruism should become highly valued by the children. These principles are more than the tenets of raising normal children; they provide a prescription for treatment of children who have failed to learn these values.

Adults working with such children need to discard the distance they often develop from them in maintaining a sense of authority. Rather, they must learn to build relationships that can break through the children's attitudes of suspiciousness, distrust, and defiance. Attachment is seen as a powerful, innate need in children. In order to form relationships, the adult must convey caring, knowledge of the feelings of the child, respect, and willingness to meet the child's needs. Even the most "unlovable" child must be afforded these qualities. Workers need to resist being lured into patterns of counter-aggression that would fulfill the child's expectations about adults.

Counseling with children is often immediate, when a situation occurs, rather than in formal counseling sessions. Focus is placed upon teaching inner controls and values rather than external punishment. Brendtro, Brokenleg, and Van Bockern also recommend mobilizing the power of peers, encouraging youth leadership and experience in working with a troubled child. In this way, they express optimism in creating a new generation of children based on enduring values and a heritage of caring. An attempt to expand and operationalize these ideas is found in Chapter 12.

## *CRITICISM*

Pelton (1989; 1991) has been an outspoken critic of the Child Welfare System in the United States as being ineffective in bringing about "permanency" planning and outcomes. Pelton points out that the permanency movement became a major facet of the federal Adoption Assistance and Child Welfare Act (AACWA) of 1980 (Public Law 96-272). The underlying philosophy of the act is that every child has a right to a permanent and stable home, preferably his or her own, and that a plan should be made for every child in foster care for a more permanent living arrangement. Rather, Pelton asserts, the Child Welfare System has fostered a revolving-door, foster placement system focusing exclusively on those children already in foster care and is doing little to provide prevention of foster placements and preservation of the family. He criticizes social workers as being unnecessarily involved in the investigatory and placement process, which he says should be left to the police and the courts. For the half-million children in foster care, he feels there has been too much of an emphasis upon blaming parents and removing children. Most incidents of injury and alleged abuse, he asserts, are related to factors of poverty and represent accidental situations better handled by counseling, education, and support, rather than removal. Rather than perpetuating the present system, Pelton urges social workers to emulate the role of visiting nurses or the old settlement houses in providing a truly helping role, quoting Jane Addams: "The only really popular charity is that of the visiting nurses, who by virtue of their professional training render services which may easily be interpreted into sympathy and kindness, ministering as they do to obvious needs which do not require investigation" (Addams, 1916, p. 26). Although Pelton's criticisms of the present system may be valid, his solutions have evoked their own criticisms and are controversial (Barth, 1993). The next chapter examines the use of foster care placements and their effectiveness more closely.

# Chapter 2

# Foster Care

"Most kids taken from their homes go to foster placements, right?"

"Yes, foster homes were intended to be short term and a transition back to the natural home. It hasn't worked out that way."

"So you guys get the foster home failures?"

"Very often. And sometimes we need to refer children to foster homes after they leave us."

"So what are you accomplishing?"

"They might not have been able to adjust to a foster placement before the RTF placement. Sometimes we can help locate a suitable foster placement."

"And sometimes I guess you provide just another stop in an endless sequence of holding stations."

"Unfortunately, yes."

"It seems far more preferable to send children to a foster home than to a larger residential setting."

"I would think so too. But remember, these children bring a lot of baggage with them. They bring the influences of their natural family to the new family and react to the new family in ways they have learned from their natural family. They may feel guilty about relating to a new set of parents. Often they reject the concept of another family. Children have to be ready for such a placement—to distance themselves somewhat from their real parents. Some children cannot tolerate the closeness. Sometimes the fault is with the foster parents seeking something in the relationship that the child cannot provide."

"So how do you decide?"

"Often by the seat of our pants. We try to weed out families wanting foster children for the wrong reasons. Probably every child could be placed successfully in a foster situation if the match with the family was right. I don't know what the parameters are. We will soon be licensed for therapeutic foster care. Perhaps we'll find out."

\* \* \*

Of the estimated half-million children nationally in out-of-home care (Cimons, 1989), more than 360,000 are foster youth (Barden, 1991), the majority as a result of abuse and neglect. This chapter reviews the history of foster care in this country, describes the needs and characteristics of both foster children and foster families, presents some model programs, examines the effectiveness of foster care, and summarizes the global needs of the foster care system. Although this book focuses more specifically on larger, more restrictive residential treatment facilities, this chapter is included as a general background against which residential treatment may be evaluated. Many children who are referred to RTFs have already had numerous failed foster placements. Others might better be placed in foster care but homes are not available for them. Foster homes may serve as a "step down" for many children in residential treatment centers.

By the end of the nineteenth century, there was growing concern over parental neglect and abuse. The Society for Prevention of Cruelty to Children was granted powers by the courts to remove children from homes that were judged to be unsuitable and to place them in alternative homes. "Boarding out" became accepted in eastern cities. Older children were placed in "free" homes and were expected to work to earn their keep. Younger children were not expected to work. Boarding payments began to become available to ensure the placement of hard-to-place children. Although boarding-out arrangements grew in popularity over free homes (placing out), they were still less frequently used than orphanages, even as late as the 1930s. The growth of the juvenile court system accelerated the growth of boarding homes for children who came under court supervision.

Creation of Title IV of the Social Security Act of 1935 (Aid to Dependent Children) allowed for the financial involvement of state governments and tipped the balance in favor of foster homes, and by 1960, there were almost twice as many children in foster care as in institutions (Hasci, 1995), reaching a peak in the late 1970s. Amendments to the Social Security Act (Titles IV-B and XX) created federal matching funds for children placed in foster care. In 1980, the federal Adoption Assistance and Child Welfare Act targeted money for preventive services and family reunification efforts. Emphasis in the legislation was placed on keeping families together whenever possible and, if children had to be removed, reuniting them as quickly as possible. As mentioned in Chapter 1, Pelton (1989; 1991) has been an outstanding critic of the removal of children, attributing causes to poverty more than to poor parenting. Although dropping in the 1970s and 1980s, the number of children in foster care has risen rapidly over the past decade. Hasci (1995) notes that the children now coming into foster care are poorer, younger, and more troubled than those in the past.

## CHARACTERISTICS AND NEEDS
## OF FOSTER CHILDREN

Not the least of the debilitating effects of frequent foster home placements is the impact upon the child's functioning in school. Ayasse (1995) points out that such changes also result in changes in school assignments, with consequent problems in adjusting to new educational expectations and requirements, new curricula, and the need to make new friends. A study by the Children's Services Division of the State of Oregon (White, Carrington, and Freeman, 1990) found that children with multiple foster home placements were less likely to be performing at or above grade level and were less involved in extracurricular activities than children who had more stable school placements. One reason for this discrepancy is the failure of case managers to track educational needs in any consistent fashion (Ayasse, 1995). When children change schools, records of their special education needs and learning disabilities often stay with the prior home or school.

As might be expected, children with multiple foster home placements suffer disproportionately from emotional disturbance (Goerge et al., 1992), behavioral problems (Marcus, 1991), and lower self-esteem (Lyman and Bird, 1996). Histories of neglect and abuse and patterns of aggressive and disruptive behaviors are similar to those described earlier for children being referred for residential treatment.

Although numerous studies document the fact that children in foster care have psychological problems, little research has been performed specifically on sexually abused children in foster care. One exception is a report of two studies by Thompson, Authier, and Ruma (1994) in which foster parents assessed the problems of sexually abused children placed in their care, usually for their own protection. In the first study, 300 foster parents completed a questionnaire. Among the problems reported as "very bothersome," at least 40 percent of the ratings were running away, suicide threats, suicide attempts, seductive behavior in the foster family, unreasonable fears, seductive behavior with peers, promiscuous behavior, compulsive masturbation, exposure of private parts, self-mutilation, and use of drugs and alcohol. Other behaviors rated "sometimes" or "frequently" were clinging behavior, sleep problems, school problems, physical complaints, aggressive behaviors, eating problems, nightmares, bed-wetting, and running away.

A second study was completed during foster family training sessions, with seventy-three parents participating. One parent from each family rated a foster child in their care. Thirty-three children were rated, ranging in age from four to seventeen. The Achenbach Child Behavior Checklist was used as the rating instrument (Achenbach, 1991a). This scale yields ratings on four broad-band factors: total social competence (e.g., social relationships), internalizing behavior problems (e.g., depression, anxiety), externalizing behavior problems (e.g., hyperactivity, aggression), and total behavior problems. Over 75 percent of the children rated scored in the borderline or clinical ranges for each of the four factors as compared with 16 percent of a normative sample. The consistency of these two studies attests to the challenges faced by foster parents of sexually abused children.

## CHARACTERISTICS AND NEEDS
## OF FOSTER FAMILIES

Dillon (1994) analyzes the complex social and cultural attitudes that may impede the successful adjustment of African-American foster children into African-American or white families. African-American children represent about 70 percent of the children in out-of-home care (Tatara, 1992). Dillon points out that there is a tendency to perceive African Americans as an undifferentiated, homogeneous group when, in fact, diverse feelings and attitudes exist among African Americans. An accurate assessment of foster families insofar as a "match" with a foster child must be sensitive to this diversity.

African Americans differ among themselves in the degree to which they internalize dominant (in this country) European attitudes and seek acculturation as opposed to seeking self-definition stemming from their original cultural roots. The degree of blackness of the child, the potential foster family, and even the worker trying to help may be either a significant aid or an impediment to a successful placement. The sensitive worker will need to consider such differences in feelings and attitudes since they become predictors of future family stability. Dillon points out that a disproportionate amount of so-called "beautiful" African Americans have Caucasian features. African-American children, foster parents, and workers may reject placements more because of internalized white racist attitudes that arouse self-hate than because of objective factors in the placement situation. Dillon's article does not advocate for limiting placements on the basis of similarity between the child and the foster family. Rather, the foster family needs to be sensitive to diversity and to allow room for the child to develop according to his or her own needs, rather than to "transform" the child according to some stereotyped ideal standard.

One way of looking at foster families is to examine personality profiles of those judged to be effective and compare them with their less effective counterparts. This type of approach may be productive in identifying the characteristics of parents that can be used to predict the effectiveness of foster care.

Although problems in children such as aggressiveness and school and peer problems are correlated with unsuccessful care, there is a dearth of research related to effectiveness of foster care. Ray and Horner (1990) report one such study in which the personality characteristics of fourteen pairs of foster parents were studied and related to their effectiveness in parenting emotionally disturbed, sexually abused children. Personality characteristics were assessed using the 16PF, a personality inventory (Krug, 1983). Sixteen bipolar personality traits and four second-order profile scales are assessed by this instrument. Foster parent effectiveness was defined by both objective (e.g., duration of the placement and unplanned removal of the child) and subjective ratings by caseworkers or researchers. The foster parent group differed from general population norms, with higher frequencies of moderate scores on all four second-order factors: extroversion, anxiety, tough poise, and independence.

According to Ray and Horner, this pattern reflects more balanced functioning on such factors as introversion-extraversion and internal-external locus of control. Furthermore, foster parent couples were more similar to each other than those in the general population, more conservative in their values, more creative, and more self-disciplined than the general population. There were also significant correlations between personality factors and effective foster parenting. Moderate scores on the four second-order factors were positively correlated with effectiveness ratings. Individual personality traits also correlated significantly with parenting effectiveness, although the correlations were low. More effective parenting was correlated with less personality similarity between the two parents.

Because of the small sample size, conclusions drawn are considered tentative. Further research with larger samples is clearly called for, as well as examination of personality matches with the foster children in successful and unsuccessful foster placements.

### *Some Model Programs*

A number of optimistic descriptions of model foster family programs are available. These typically take the form of "treatment foster family" ("therapeutic foster family") homes with various therapeutic services "wrapped around" a traditional foster family placement. Some of these accounts present outcome data; others do not. These programs are seen as an alternative to residential treatment in larger group settings. The issue of effectiveness of foster family or therapeutic foster family placement is considered below.

Therapeutic foster care (TFC) is considered necessary for children requiring placement who have serious emotional disturbances.

It is seen as a more acceptable alternative to residential treatment in a larger, congregate living facility. It represents a combination of child welfare and mental health approaches. The foster family is used to provide normal, family-living experiences with professional services being "wrapped around." As with other child welfare programs operating under CASSP principles, family reunification is the ultimate goal.

For some foster care programs, the goal is a stable placement until the child reaches the age of majority. In such cases, presumably, there is little likelihood of return to the biological family, and the foster parents serve in a similar capacity as adoptive parents. In some cases, they may actually elect to adopt the child. In other programs, the goal, as with residential treatment facilities, is to return children to the biological family.

An example of the first type is a program administered by Hope for the Children (Azar, 1995), which provides long-term and often permanent homes for foster children in Illinois. The homes are clustered in an experimental community in a residential neighborhood. The program keeps siblings together and attempts to give foster parents the same rights as adoptive parents, allowing them to adopt the child if he or she becomes legally available. The program, developed by psychologist Brenda Krause Eheart, is intended to provide the child with at least one caring adult who will provide a stable environment in a safe, multiracial, multigenerational community.

To add to the support provided the children, the program provides low-rent housing to forty-five senior citizens who volunteer in the program. The seniors volunteer six to eight hours a week to spend time with the children, baby-sit, work in local schools, and take a general interest in the program. Hope for Children screens and trains parents and attempts to secure effective matches between parent and child based on evaluations of lifestyles and personalities. The support network provided foster parents is unique in the national foster family system.

A British program (Bradley and Aldgate, 1994) illustrates a short-term respite approach to foster care; there is no question that the children will return to their original families. The program "takes the heat off" families in severe need or crisis, allowing them a breathing space to strengthen their coping strategies. Bradley and Aldgate provide no information about the duration of "short-term" arrangements, but the placement was generally designed to help the family through a difficult coping situation. "Carers" received six to eight training sessions and lived within fifteen miles of the family. Their task was child oriented. They interacted with the family generally only at regular "review" meetings. Carers received advice and support from a family placement social worker. New carers were sometimes linked in formal "buddy" systems with experienced carers, and they often established informal support systems with family and friends. They were expected to handle child behavior problems such as bed-wetting, sleep disturbances, and aggression.

While no data is provided, Bradley and Aldgate attribute successful relationships to carer sensitivity to the cultural background of the family and the real circumstances that necessitated placement such as poverty, housing, physical or mental health problems. Unsuccessful placements seemed to relate to conflicts between the family and the carer. Difficulties arose from excessive dependency on the carer and ambivalence on the part of the carer toward the family.

A program that does provide outcome data is administered by Lutheran Social Services in Spokane, Washington. The Sexually Reactive Youth Program (Ray et al., 1995) provides residential care using therapeutic foster parents for children below the age of thirteen who have been both victims of sexual abuse and are sexually abusing other children. Treatment is typically of eighteen months duration but sometimes lasts longer. Specially trained foster parents provide home-based behavioral interventions to the children. Their efforts are supplemented by psychiatric aides who provide behavior management, crisis intervention, supportive counseling, socialization, and supervision. A broader treatment team includes teachers, probation officers, physicians, and the natural parents if the child is to return home. Individual and group education and counseling are provided to the child, and family counseling is available to the natural and foster family.

The most important goal of the program is the cessation of inappropriate sexual behavior. The program utilizes a risk assessment matrix related to sexual abuse, with nine items rated on a five-point scale according to level of abuse. Items included are level of aggression, level of sophistication and preplanning, level of coercion, level of empathy, escalation in occurrences, resistance to treatment, denial of responsibility, social skills, and knowledge of age-appropriate sexual behavior.

Outcome data are reported for fifteen children with a mean age of ten years. Eight of the nine variables on the risk assessment matrix showed a statistically significant change after one year of treatment.

An intensive treatment foster care program has been developed by the Oregon Social Learning Center (Moore and Chamberlain, 1994) for adolescents who are at risk for incarceration in group homes because of delinquency. The goal is to provide community-based treatment in a relatively nonrestrictive setting where youths will not be separated from nondisabled peers or isolated from their families. The program derives from an extension of the social interaction theory and treatment model elaborated by Gerald Patterson and his colleagues (Patterson, Chamberlain, and Reid, 1982) to deal with conduct disorders, aggression, and delinquency.

The program follows a seven-component model that includes foster parent recruitment and screening, preservice training, ongoing consultation with professional staff, school consultation and monitoring of behavioral and academic progress, weekly individual therapy, family therapy, and after-care, wraparound services for families. Among the unique aspects of the program is a $100 finder's fee to foster parents for recruiting new families. A twenty- to thirty-hour training period for families teaches social-learning principles, limit setting, specific daily teaching techniques, and a point-and-level system to provide reinforcements and consequences for behavior. Daily telephone consultations using a parent report checklist of problem behaviors and twenty-four-hour crisis intervention are also an innovative part of the program. There are weekly group meetings for foster parents and a daily school report card carried by the child and completed by teachers. Project staff are also available to intervene in the classroom if needed.

From the perspective of a behaviorally oriented psychologist, the Oregon program seems to be the Cadillac of therapeutic treatment. It must also be an enormously expensive program (cost figures are not provided), beyond the range of feasibility in other than funded research and university settings.

Mention should also be made here of the increasing use of "relative foster care" or "kinship care" as an alternative for abused and neglected children (Gleeson, 1995). This raises concerns about distinguishing family responsibilities from government responsibilities in protecting children. To what extent should government intrude into kinship networks and what are the financial responsibilities of government and extended family members? Increasingly, states are using relatives for substitute care arrangements, providing the same financial support to relatives as to nonrelated foster parents and attempting to regulate these homes in the same way as ordinary foster homes.

The number of children placed with relatives by child welfare agencies is rapidly approaching the number of children in nonrelated foster homes. Children in kinship care are likely to remain in care much longer, to be African American, and to live in major urban centers. They are less likely to be adopted than children in nonrelated homes. Most of the parents involved with the child welfare system for these children are mothers, while most of the caregivers are grandmothers. Nearly all of the birth families and caregivers are very poor. Since child welfare has been castigated for failing to provide culturally relevant services to the children in out-of-home placements, kinship care may partially satisfy these objections. However, it has also been pointed out that kinship caregivers, reflecting populations that are also at risk, may fail to provide the empowerment and self-determination mandated by foster care programs. Others maintain (e.g., Meyer and Link, 1990) that perpetrators of abuse may have easier access to children in kinship care than in nonrelated homes.

## EFFECTIVENESS OF FOSTER CARE

In 1995, Speaker of the House Newt Gingrich attacked the foster care system in this country as a failure and called for the reintroduction of orphanages to ensure stability of placement for children removed from their natural homes. Few would agree with return to orphanages as a solution but the fact that foster care, originally designed as a short-term solution leading to return to families or permanent adoption, has not lived up to its promise cannot be denied. Less than 40 percent of children who remain in foster care longer than two years will return home. Infants and toddlers make up the largest percentage of children referred for foster home placements. Many of these children are born to substance abusers and remain in foster care. There is a shortage of foster parents so those parents who do serve in this capacity are asked to take larger numbers of children. Twenty percent of children living in runaway shelters come directly from foster homes. Eighty percent of prisoners in Illinois spent time in foster care as children (Azar, 1995). Despite these bleak statistics, there is some evidence that children who experience therapeutic foster care may have positive outcomes.

Galaway, Nutter, and Hudson (1995) review nine research studies in Canada, England, and the United States focusing on seriously emotionally and behaviorally disturbed children treated in therapeutic foster care (TFC) programs. These studies suggest the children tend to meet their treatment goals, experience positive changes in self-esteem, and move on to less restrictive settings, as compared with children discharged from institutional settings. TFC programs are also less costly than institutional and group home placements. Unfortunately, these findings are not definitive. The children studied are few in number. There was no attempt to equate severity of the emotional or behavioral problems with placement success. It seems likely that children originally referred to institutional or group home care were more severely disturbed and could not be placed in foster care. Nor have there been studies that relate specific components of the therapeutic foster care programs to outcomes.

A survey of North American TFC programs (Galaway, Nutter, and Hudson, 1995) was able to relate program characteristics to two outcome variables—planned versus unplanned discharge and discharge to a more versus less restrictive setting. Questionnaires were returned from 430 programs meeting minimum criteria of therapeutic foster care. Eleven program characteristics were studied for 1,500 discharged young people. As might be expected, there was a strong association between the two outcome variables. Eighty percent of the planned discharges and only 37 percent of the unplanned discharges were made to less restrictive living arrangements. Preadolescents were more likely to be discharged on a planned basis than were adolescents.

None of the associations between program characteristics and the two outcome variables were very strong. The program characteristics included annual per bed cost, extent of the social worker caseload for the child, private versus public or profit versus nonprofit auspices of the agency, amount of foster parent training, and the use of a specific treatment approach. However, youth discharged on a planned basis were more likely to be enrolled in high-cost, low-caseload programs. These variables did not relate significantly with restrictiveness of postdischarge living arrangements. Because of these disappointing results, Gallaway, Nutter, and Hudson urge caution in unqualified acceptance of such program characteristics as standards for therapeutic foster care. They acknowledge that the two outcome variables used are crude measures and that further research is demanded.

Clark and colleagues (1994) report on a comparative study of outcomes in two groups of 132 emotionally disturbed children and adolescents, aged seven to fifteen. The first group received "individualized" services consisting of a strength-based assessment, life-domain planning, clinical case management, and follow-along supports and services. Family-centered, clinical case managers and home-based counselors collaborated with foster care caseworkers and other providers such as therapists, scout leaders, and teachers. The second (control) group of children received whatever standard procedures were typically used in the state.

Children were randomly assigned to one of the two groups that did not differ significantly on a number of descriptive variables. The subjects had spent an average of 2.6 years in out-of-home placements and had an average annualized rate of 3.8 placement changes. Outcome data were collected from a number of sources by trained interviewers. The Child Behavior Checklist (Achenbach, 1991a) and the Youth Self-Report (Achenbach, 1991b) were among the data collected along with out-of-home placement information from client records. The formal instruments provide measures of problem areas on eight subscales (withdrawn, somatic complaints, anxious/depressed, social problems, thought problems, attention problems, delinquent behavior, and aggressive behavior). The scales yield second-order scores on two subgroupings—internalizing and externalizing.

All children participated in the study for a fifteen-month period. Data were collected at the time of entrance to the study and eighteen months later. No significant differences were found between the groups initially on the scales of emotional and behavioral adjustment, but there was a significant treatment interaction with time as a variable. The treatment group showed greater improvement than the control on all subscales. There were also significantly fewer placement changes, runaways, jail detentions, and felonies after entrance to the study in the treatment group. Long-term analysis of the stability of permanency placements and emotional adjustment was not performed.

The findings, then, are paradoxical. In general, foster care as a national program and mandate has not lived up to its promise. The original goals and directions for family preservation, for the most part, have not been met. Yet, studies of individualized programs providing a range of therapeutic and professional service yield positive and optimistic results compared with traditional foster services or institutional care. It seems that additional dollars and competent management of services may be well worth the expense and effort.

## SYSTEM NEEDS

Despite its failure to meet expectations, foster care will likely be the major strategy of the child welfare system. Hope for the future should derive from what research and experience suggest to be the most effective directions to follow. Unfortunately, practice does not always follow from research. The enormous volume of foster care literature may paradoxically act as a deterrent. It is unrealistic to believe that child welfare workers can keep abreast of the hundreds of publications covering even the most recent years.

Two British workers have attempted to link research and practice in a review article listing what appear to be the most reasonable conclusions to be drawn from the research literature (Nissim and Simm, 1994). They identify four key factors that they believe should be incorporated into practice guidelines: the age of the child at placement, contact with the family of origin, length of time in care, and behavioral problems. The first two factors are related to positive outcomes, the last two, to negative outcomes. Abstracting from their paper, the following generalizations are drawn:

- It is advantageous for the child to experience normal family life in their birth family.
- If removal from the birth family is necessary, younger children placed into foster homes have more positive outcomes.
- Contact with family of origin leads to better outcomes.
- Family links need to be actively maintained, including fathers, siblings, and grandparents.
- The greater the length of time in care, the greater the risk of negative outcome. Therefore, speedy return home should be a priority. Long stays in care should be avoided if possible.
- Behavioral problems lead to negative outcomes. Placement of children with emotional and behavioral problems without incorporating resources for identifying and treating such problems increases the risk of further problems. Therapeutic foster care programs will need to be more frequently used.

These findings and the recommendations that derive from them are based on a continuing need to identify the risk factors associated with foster placement. They emphasize the importance of family and social factors that extend beyond the problems manifested by the children.

## *FOSTER KIDS DON'T SAY "THANK YOU"*

The following information is derived from an interview conducted as part of a needs assessment with foster parents, providers, hospitals, and agencies dealing with foster children. Mrs. W. is a foster mother for Luke, formerly a resident at the RTF. She has been a foster mother since 1969 to 110 foster children. She works through the County Children and Youth Agency.

Luke is classified as a "special needs" child because of his behavioral and emotional problems. It is Mrs. W.'s understanding that medically fragile and mentally retarded children would also be designated as special needs children. Because of this classification, she receives the highest per diem rate for Luke of $35 per day. It is her belief that in her county the rate is $15 for infants and children and $25 for adolescents. Her rate is inclusive for food and clothing. It does not include medical expenses or transportation. Mrs. W. indicates that this is a fair rate which covers her expenses for Luke. Although her program is not identified as therapeutic foster care, it essentially follows that model since Luke also receives twenty hours per week of wraparound services.

Mrs. W. first became a foster parent after responding to a newspaper advertisement. She has been with the C&Y agency since 1973. Except for a very brief period of time, she has had at least one foster child since then. She is generally positive about her relationship with C&Y.

Mrs. W. indicates that many parents and C&Y workers do not understand that a foster child is not like a natural child. She has often been told to raise her foster children in the same way that she treats her natural children. This, she says, is naive. Foster children do not love you as a natural child no matter how much you do for them. Many foster parents become hurt and disillusioned because the foster child does not "give back" emotionally. Parents who go into foster care to meet their own emotional needs will be disappointed. Mrs. W. has said, "Foster children don't say 'thank you.'"

In order to be selected as a foster parent, C&Y did a family study of her financial situation, church, and school relationships. However, they do not watch too closely now. Her recent divorce had no bearing on her relationship with the agency. C&Y also "looked the other way" regarding foster care regulations since she had as many as nine children at one time in the home, including her natural children. Typically, she has had three to five foster children at one time.

In retrospect, Mrs. W. is not sure she would become as involved with teenage foster children again, knowing what she knows today. Although she did not realize it at the time, foster children did harm her natural children. They frequently stole their clothing and jewelry and were verbally abusive to her children. Mrs. W. would consider taking infants and babies into her home.

Mrs. W. feels that she has not gotten a great deal of therapeutic support from C&Y. There were times when she needed help with transportation and did not receive it. Therapeutic services are available through the local mental health/mental retardation (MH/MR) agency. There is also a crisis center in her county where she can go in an emergency.

Mrs. W. is very positive about the training she has received, especially recently. She has benefited from a competency-based training curriculum developed by a local university and being piloted in her county. It is her impression that the state wants to make this training available throughout the state. The training includes therapy issues, dealing with abused children, and drug abuse. The county also provides a Systematic Training for Effective Parenting (STEP) program of training.

Initially, Mrs. W. was asked to keep a "life book," consisting of medical records, photographs, and critical incidents. This was intended to be passed along to the next foster family. Since she does not intend to give up Luke until he is nineteen years old, she no longer maintains this record. Mrs. W. will not keep Luke beyond age nineteen, saying, "I will not allow myself to be abused by an adult."

Mrs. W. does not attend any family support groups for foster parents although she was instrumental in organizing such groups for the county in the past. She said it is difficult to motivate foster parents to attend such groups, even though they are helpful, because of time constraints. The foster parents need to be with the children. Support groups tend to be gripe sessions. Although the agency professionals who organize such groups try to prevent gripe sessions from occurring, Mrs. W. feels they are important. Foster parents walk away feeling better after they have vented their concerns with one another. She has not had time or interest to be involved with the state parents' group.

The C&Y agency does not get involved with Luke's school. They leave that to Mrs. W., and she assumes that responsibility. Luke has had no contact with his biological family. The agency controls visitations and will not allow visits. Nor can the family telephone Luke. At one time he interacted with a brother but did not know it was his brother until he was later told.

In almost all cases, foster kids stayed with Mrs. W. for twelve to eighteen months. These were mostly children and teenagers, and most returned to their families. A second group were infants and babies whom she had from birth until they were adopted at six to nine months of age. Although the children mostly returned home, it did not last. Without the child in the house, the family was functioning better; they became more confident about handling the child until the child returned, and then things often deteriorated again and another foster placement was needed. In some cases, it was back to the same foster home. Mrs. W. feels that long-term foster care is often needed. In those cases, the need should be identified early so as to avoid torturing the family and the child. Most of the children she had as foster children had multiple previous placements. Many of the foster placements failed because families did not know how to deal with teenage rebellion.

## FOSTER CARE AGENCIES

A telephone interview was conducted with A. B., case manager at Goodplace, a therapeutic foster care agency. Goodplace is a private, national agency. The rate of reimbursement at Goodplace is $121 per day through Medical Assistance. This breaks down to $109 for the therapeutic component and $12 for room and board. Most of their referrals are from Children and Youth agencies. The counties pay the room and board, but in some instances, it is paid through Supplemental Security Income (SSI) if that is available. That payment seems to be sufficient to run their program. Because of this arrangement, they have no need to use wraparound services.

Foster parents are called teaching parents. They receive three days of preservice training and then one day per month after beginning as foster parents. The training components include positive approaches to discipline and motivation, treatment and use of consequences, and sexual abuse. Teaching parents are selected through advertising.

The goal of the program is family reunification or discharge to a less restrictive setting. Many of its children may wind up in RTFs or psychiatric hospitals. Goodplace's agency in Philadelphia serves about seventy-five children. They try to place only one child per home. Only three homes have two children. They also need additional homes because they provide the mentor respite two days a month. Its staff consists of case managers (MSWs or BSWs) and clinical coordinators (MSWs). They have no psychologists but do have one part-time psychiatrist. The case managers have a caseload of eight children. The clinical coordinator has a dual role as case manager as well as the supervisor of other case managers. A.B. believes this is very difficult, and one role may compromise the other.

Crisis intervention is a major aspect of the job of case manager and clinical coordinator. It is a common occurrence for these staff members to be called out in the middle of the night. Sometimes another home must be found at this time and the child relocated. No support groups are being run at present. In the past, there were such groups, but they have disbanded.

# Chapter 3

# Diagnosing Behavioral
# and Emotional Disorders

"So, does your program follow a medical model?"

"We are governed by Department of Health regulations as well as those of the Department of Public Welfare so, to some extent, we do. Regulations require an Axis I psychiatric diagnosis. Medications are based upon such a diagnosis, although the system is imperfect. Treatment goals should also be consistent with diagnosis, yet I know we often fail to do so."

"Why is diagnosis so important anyway? We both know it tends to be unreliable. It's only an abstraction and probably has little relationship to what you actually do with the children. If a child is aggressive, you treat the aggressive behavior. Why worry about superfluous labels?"

"Come now, I know you know better than that. Sure there is unreliability, but the field is constantly improving the classification system. That's why etiology was left out of the diagnostic process. Only observable behaviors are considered, and these are fairly rigidly defined. If the label brings order from chaos, it adds something."

"OK, I'll grant you that, but what about the stigmatizing effects? You call a child schizophrenic and it sticks with him. Labels may have some value in easing the anxieties of the shrinks, but what does it do for the child? You know as well as I do that these diagnoses have surplus meaning, even if it is inaccurate. Look at the terms 'idiot' and 'imbecile.' They also had scientific value at one time. Then they became pejoratives. They still have that connotation a century later and are not used at all in diagnosis."

"Pretty clever. Yes, these labels acquire surplus emotional meaning. The old study by Schacter and Singer (1962) demonstrated that cognitions can influence emotions and behaviors. Inject adrenalin into a subject and give him social clues that he is angry and he will report being angry. Make someone else feel that he is in a fun situation and he will report feeling happy. Both subjects are experiencing the same physiological arousal. What they tell themselves seems to influence what they feel. I suppose diagnostic labels might have the same effect in generating negative feelings toward persons described by certain labels."

"So, you finally admit I'm right."

"There's a risk in using labels, yes . . . but I'm not ready to abandon diagnoses. We don't stop using antibiotics because they might produce unpleasant side effects. We do try to reduce the side effects or find a medicine that doesn't produce any. People need to be educated. That's why all the emphasis is being placed on using politically correct labels. Diagnosis counts. Mental health professionals need to make it more precise and more reliable."

*    *    *

The process of classifying emotional disorders derives from a medical model. Before a physical disease is treated, the symptoms are described and classified into a system of syndromes related on one hand to known or presumed etiology and on the other to a treatment with proven efficacy in alleviating that disease or condition. There may be errors or misinformation about the etiology, and treatments may prove to be ineffective, but the process should be self-correcting based upon empirical evidence. In a similar manner, the treatment of emotional problems derives from this approach.

Earlier conceptions of mental illness included concepts derived from magic, religion, and superstition. Modern-day treatments no longer rely upon exorcism, orgone boxes, or magnetism. We no longer burn witches at the stake for mental derangement just as we have given up bleeding with leeches to treat high fever. Yet these methods made sense at one time and were seemingly logical extensions of elaborate belief systems. Diagnosis and classification provide order from chaos and provide a conceptual basis for treatment.

In the seventeenth and eighteenth centuries, mental illness and mental retardation were poorly delineated. With finer distinctions drawn between these conditions, treatment also became more differentiated. Today, diagnosis of emotional disorder is closely related to treatment options and provides the basis for statistical and research investigations expanding our knowledge base.

The process of diagnosis is not, however, without its critics. Labels tend to stigmatize and they remain with the child. The various diagnoses have images associated with them that may be negative and harmful to the child. The diagnosis of "conduct disorder," for example, described below, may exclude children from certain placements. Some psychiatrists are, therefore, reluctant to use this diagnosis, using the more benign "oppositional defiant disorder" or "adjustment disorder" instead. As with any abstraction, a diagnostic classification tends to make us equate two children labeled in the same way as if they were identical, blurring individual differences, which may be far more significant than the similarities.

Diagnoses are meaningful only insofar as they clarify the behavior, relate to some etiology, and point the way to effective treatment. Finally, psychiatric diagnosis is notoriously unreliable. It is not uncommon to find, in reviewing a child's chart, that numerous diagnoses have been applied over a period of time. Different hospitals, treatment centers, and practitioners apply certain diagnoses more frequently than others. Funding and political considerations also play a role in what label is being applied.

The DSM series of diagnosis and classification manuals (*Diagnostic and Statistical Manual of Mental Disorders*) developed by the American Psychiatric Association periodically updates and improves criteria for diagnosis. Etiological considerations were removed from the process since these are often unclear. We are currently using DSM-IV (American Psychiatric Association, 1994). This manual provides very precise criteria for differential diagnosis, with lengthy lists of behaviors and symptoms that must be present for a diagnosis to apply. Nevertheless, the process remains subjective and is often not terribly reliable.

DSM-IV uses a multiaxial approach to diagnosis. The individual is given a label on each of five axes. Axis 1 is the axis for a mental health disorder and is the primary diagnosis of emotional disturbance. It includes conduct disorders, ADHD, schizophrenia, anxiety disorders, and mood disorders, as well as various other constellations of symptoms and behaviors presumed to occur on an emotional basis. In order to be accepted (and funded) in a residential treatment facility for emotional disturbance the child must have an Axis 1 diagnosis. Axis 2 is used for developmental disorders such as mental retardation, as well as long-term personality or characterological disorders such as "borderline personality." Children with both an Axis 1 diagnosis and an Axis 2 mental retardation disorder are considered dually diagnosed. Axis 3 is reserved for medical conditions that may be contributing to the overall problem. Axis 4 lists the environmental stressors that may be contributory, such as marital conflict between the parents or parental abuse. Axis 5 is a global rating of overall adjustment expressed as a number on a scale ranging from 1 to 100.

In DSM-IV several conditions involve disruptive behavior. Attention Deficit Hyperactivity Disorder (ADHD) is used for persons with inappropriate degrees of inattention, impulsiveness, and hyperactivity. Children diagnosed with ADHD appear to have their engines turned up too high. It occurs in about 3 percent of the population and is six to nine times more common in boys than girls. Such children have problems in school because of their inattentiveness, although learning disability may not be a necessary characteristic. Children with ADHD are more active, restless, and fidgety than normal children. They have more difficulty adhering to rules and instructions. ADHD often occurs in conjunction with other psychiatric disorders such as anxiety and depression. Treatment typically utilizes structured behavior modification procedures as well as the use of stimulants such as Ritalin that decrease hyperactivity. The condition persists throughout childhood and may result in antisocial behaviors in adulthood.

Oppositional Defiant Disorder (ODD) is a label used to describe negativistic, hostile, and defiant behaviors without more serious violations of the rights of others. Such children tend to be argumentative and rebellious. They curse and display tantrum behaviors. They deliberately defy adult requests, rules, and regulations and consistently provoke and blame others for their difficulties. ODD often occurs concurrently with ADHD.

Children with Conduct Disorder display all the characteristics of Oppositional Defiant Disorder, but their defiance is more serious. They consistently violate the rights of others as well as accepted societal norms. Physical aggression is common. They may deliberately demonstrate cruelty to animals or other people. They may destroy property, set fires, or engage in lying, cheating, or stealing. They are truant from school and may run away from home. As they grow older, they may become prone to rape, assault, armed robbery, and even homicide. They have little concern for the feelings of others and appear to demonstrate no remorse for their misdeeds.

Numerous writers have associated antisocial behavior in children with characteristics of the parents and family. Parents of antisocial youths are more likely themselves to suffer from various psychiatric disorders, alcoholism, and criminal behavior. They tend to be harsh in their attitudes and disciplinary practices. Children with conduct disorder are more likely than others to have been victims of abuse. There is a likelihood of discrepancy in parental disciplinary strategies, e.g., severe punishment by the father and lax discipline by the mother. Prosocial behavior tends to be ignored or even punished. Parents of such children are less likely to monitor their child's whereabouts and may, purposefully or unwittingly, reward aggressive behavior. They provide less warmth and emotional support than parents of normal youths. Marital discord, family dysfunction, and divorce occur more frequently.

## DEPRESSION AND SUICIDE

It should not be surprising to mental health professionals that children become depressed. Yet the diagnosis of depression in childhood and even adolescence may be missed because it is masked by other behaviors. Children and adolescents may not present the symptoms traditionally associated with depression in the same manner as adults. Adolescents, known to be prone to extreme mood swings, may not be detected as manifesting more serious depressive disorders. Adolescent boys may not engage in the same overt, self-destructive behaviors as girls, yet their self-exposure to dangerous and aggressive situations may be an attempt at self-annihilation. The hopelessness of children separated from families or exposed to abuse may be as much a symptom of depression and a cry for help as the more easily recognizable withdrawal of adults.

The scope of the problem can be understood by examining the epidemiology of suicide in children and adolescents. Although there is a direct correlation between suicide rate and age, a substantial number of children do commit suicide each year in this country. Suicide is nonexistent under age five and virtually nonexistent for children between the ages of five and nine. There are about 100 suicides a year for children aged ten to fourteen with an eight- to tenfold increase in children and adolescents aged fifteen to nineteen. About 15,000 college students attempt suicide each year.

The contemplation of suicide by a child rests at first upon the development of a concept of death as irreversible. This concept does not exist before the age of five. Later, children learn to use the self-infliction of pain as a means of manipulating adults and may structure relationships in that manner (Yakoubian and Lourie, 1973).

Child psychiatrists view suicidal determinants as aggression turned inwardly perhaps as punishment for guilt and social isolation and withdrawal to escape intolerable situations. Suicidal thoughts and death wishes are not uncommon even in normal developmental patterns. Most children have learned to reject the behavior as an adaptive device but may derive pleasure in contemplating the reaction of others to their death. Both developmental and environmental stress can increase the likelihood of suicide in children who may already have developed a predisposition to such behavior. Immature adolescents with poor ego development and inadequate impulse control may be particularly at risk.

Hereditary tendencies, as well as social and cultural influences, also contribute. When there is an absence of support from the environment, drug use, and lack of cohesion in the family constellation, children will be more at risk for suicidal behavior. Although cultural factors contribute, the individual dynamics of the child will determine how external stresses are handled. As with adults, "The severity of the suicidal risk can be reflected by the depth of the conflict—degree of guilt, self-castigation, helplessness, primitive quality of aggressive fantasies, and the inner and outer resources available to the adolescent" (Yakoubian and Lourie, 1973, p. 164).

## *EGO DISTURBANCE*

A number of conditions are often lumped together by psychiatrists as ego disturbances since they represent serious dysfunction in perception, memory, cognition, reality testing, and object relations. Stennis (1973) includes such diagnoses as mental retardation, organic brain syndromes, childhood psychosis, and early infantile autism. DSM-IV separates these conditions. Autism is seen as more related to Pervasive Developmental Disorder, rather than psychosis, without implications of faulty parental interactions as a determining factor. Childhood psychosis is more accurately labeled as childhood schizophrenia when there is evidence of auditory or visual hallucinations and severe disturbance in thinking and reality testing. Schizophrenic children are best treated in psychiatric hospitals during the acute phases of their syndrome but may be referred to the RTF as a "step-down" placement when they are in remission.

## ATTACHMENT AND ATTACHMENT DISORDERS

Attachment is generally defined as an enduring affectional bond of substantial intensity. The relationship between such bonds, established in infancy, has long been of interest to developmental psychologists. Bowlby (1969, 1973, 1980) has conceptualized this process of attachment to parents during infancy as critical in the ability to form interpersonal attachments at any age, and the effects of disruption of this attachment process in infancy can produce later emotional and psychological disturbance, particularly the inability to engage in trusting and secure relationships with others. Numerous authors have demonstrated the relationship between secure attachments in infancy and ego strength, peer attachments, and social competence in preschool years. Armsden and Greenberg (1987) have published reliability data on an Inventory of Parent and Peer Attachment that is useful in assessing this behavior. The relevance of such measures in assessment and treatment of adolescents in out-of-home placements seems indisputable.

## DUAL DIAGNOSIS

Mentally retarded children are best treated at home or in small residential settings geared toward teaching adaptive behaviors, often in community settings. Increasingly, it is being recognized that mentally retarded persons may also be emotionally disturbed.

The multiaxial approach of DSM-IV allows for the labeling of such "dually diagnosed" individuals. Some children with both diagnoses are being accepted in RTFs, but the diagnosis is made difficult because of the cognitive and language impairments of the children. Treatment is also complicated since there is a tendency to treat nonspecific behaviors such as aggression rather than diagnostic conditions. Many psychiatrists are not experienced in prescribing for children with dual diagnoses.

The diagnostic process is a combination of formal and informal assessment processes. Psychologists and psychiatrists may differ in specific approaches to assessment but there is overlap. As mentioned previously, DSM-IV uses current behaviors as criteria for distinguishing between syndromes. However, a clinical interview will attempt to obtain an historical account of the child's early development including school performance, serious medical conditions, and current developmental level. Psychiatrists may use some form of a mental status examination to assess cognitive functioning and developmental level. Psychologists are more thoroughly trained in the use of psychometric procedures and more likely to utilize tests of intelligence, emotional, and personality functioning.

A variety of behavior rating scales are used by both psychologists and psychiatrists. Some, such as the Achenbach (1991a, 1991b) and Conners (1997), are rough screening instruments for a variety of childhood behavior syndromes. Others are specific to certain diagnostic categories such as depression. Many psychologists are trained to use projective tests of personality to gain a better understanding of personality structure, clarity of thinking and perception, reality testing, defense mechanisms, and specific areas of conflict. The Rorschach (inkblot) test and the Thematic Apperception Test are two of the most widely used techniques.

Objective tests of personality are also employed with more established norms, reliability, and validity. Projective testing has been compared to the reception of a standard AM/FM radio. The receiver has the potential of bringing in a wide range of frequencies, but the fidelity of sound is not high. Projective tests have the potential of eliciting an infinite number of responses and, therefore, of generating an enormous range of inferences about the personality and functioning of the person being evaluated. However, the reliability and validity of the information may not be high. Test interpretation represents an art as much as a science. Objective tests, on the other hand, are more like a fine FM radio tuned only to one frequency. The radio has exceptional fidelity but there is no possibility of listening to anything but the pretuned channel. Attempts to make the Rorschach conform to the more rigid empirical requirements of a psychometric procedure (Exner and Weiner, 1982; Exner, 1986) are a possible exception to this broadcasting analogy.

It is essential in evaluating children that families be included in the overall assessment. Children cannot be studied in a vacuum. Family problems are closely interwoven into the fabric of the child's adjustment. This assertion is not limited to the situations of abuse and violence detailed in Chapter 6. For this reason, family systems approaches to assessment and treatment have great validity.

Diagnosis of mental disorders in children, as with adults, remains a somewhat controversial and often subjective enterprise. At best, diagnosis provides a set of hypotheses that may be validated or disconfirmed by treatment. If treatment options followed consistently and logically from diagnoses, the process would be more clear-cut. If a treatment strategy that derives from diagnosis (e.g., the use of Haldol for schizophrenia) does not work, it may lead to reconsideration of the diagnosis. Although this process is circular, in the final analysis, diagnosis is useful only to the degree that it leads to effective efforts at treatment or disposition.

## FAMILY ASSESSMENT

Many workers have pointed out the folly of evaluating children without a comprehensive evaluation of the family support system, including interactions between the caregiver and the child as well as between caregivers. A number of family risk, family cohesion, and family problem scales have been developed to assess the outcome of services. A comprehensive measure developed at the Children's Bureau of Los Angeles (McCroskey, Nishimoto, and Subramanian, 1991), the Family Assessment Form (FAF), is multidimensional. The instrument assesses the family's physical, social, and financial environment; the caregivers' history, personal characteristics, and child-rearing skills; the interactions among all family members; and the child's developmental status and behavior. The assessment leads to a psychosocial summary that includes overall ratings of all areas of functioning and a listing of family strengths and concerns. A treatment plan is developed from these ratings. Although the scope of the FAF is impressive, thus far, validity data are limited to content validity, and reliability assessment, to internal consistency.

# Chapter 4

# The Concept of the "Moral Imbecile"

"Have you ever considered that the behaviors you are trying to change are inborn—genetic—so that you are wasting your time? I know that we psychologists have tended to look toward environment and psychological determinants for most behavior. You know the argument. Lower organisms are biologically driven—tropisms, reflexes, and other inborn drives. But humans are above all that. We can process; we have choices. We can alter our environment, overcome our biology. Suppose it's not true. Suppose your behavior disorders are really the result of some pernicious gene passed on from generation to generation. Suppose it's irreversible even within the best environment. Aren't you just banging your head against the wall?"

"There may indeed be genetic factors involved here, or other biological determinants. Fetal alcohol syndrome affects some of the children. It seems to be associated with a number of behavioral as well as physical problems. There is increasing evidence that certain stereotyped behavior disorders are related to Tourette's Syndrome and may have genetic etiology. One researcher calls them broadband, inherited, psychiatric disorders. It has long been suspected that conduct disorder may be inherited. The mechanisms are unclear. Genes provide the blueprint for the production of proteins that drive the body's chemical reactions and serve as building blocks for body structures. They affect the production of neurotransmitters and the regulation of basic bodily processes, even the aging of cells associated with death. There is no question that genes play a role in the behaviors we encounter in these children."

"So I'm right."

"Not quite. Professionals in the field of mental retardation drew the same conclusion at the turn of the century when the basic laws

of inheritance became known. They assumed that all mental retardation was inherited and therefore irreversible; that despite the finest
educational programs, mentally retarded persons could not improve.
It set the field back fifty years. Genetics may provide limitations but
probably doesn't affect more than 50 percent of the variance in
behavioral measures. Psychotropic medications are designed to affect
neurotransmitters and may provide the brake or accelerator that can
overcome or attenuate genetic inputs."

"What you need is more powerful technology, including genetic
engineering."

"We need technology beyond behavioral techniques. You know
the ethical issues here as well as I do."

"We won't see answers here in our lifetime."

### ORIGINS OF GENETIC CONCEPT

The concept of the "moral imbecile" did not originate with mental
retardation, but it assumed particular significance in the treatment
of persons with mental retardation. The concept arose from early
value-laden judgments and implications about the etiology of
retardation in "crimes against nature" of the parents or predecessors
of the affected individual. The concept was abandoned with greater
understanding about organic determinants, learning, and social factors. More recent understanding of genetic mechanisms is in some
ways reminiscent of the original concept.

The Italian criminologist Lombrosso (1973) identified physical
stigmata of degeneration that he believed were associated with
criminality and which revealed a biological predisposition to crime.
However, the notion that criminality rests in the genes probably
derives most directly from the nineteenth-century phrenological
theories of Spurzheim (1834) and Gall (1835).* Indeed, Samuel
Gridley Howe (1848), credited with initiating the first American

---

*Sources for a discussion of phrenology and its influence upon psychology
include: Boring, E.G. (1929). *A History of Experimental Psychology.* New York:
Century, pp. 47-57; Fancher, R.R. (1990). *Pioneers of Psychology.* New York:
W.W. Norton, pp. 74-80; and Murphy, G. (1951). *Historical Introduction to Modern Psychology.* New York: Harcourt Brace, pp. 56-57.

effort in teaching children with mental retardation, was greatly influenced by these theories. Initially, moral imbecility was considered a small subset of the larger condition of mental deficiency.

In some persons, retardation affected the development of the moral sense, even when other areas of cognitive functioning were normal. Indeed, the moral imbecile with normal intelligence was most dangerous because of his ability to deceive and influence others. Later, some workers believed that *all* persons with mental retardation fell, at least potentially, into the criminal ranks. In either case, the associations among mental retardation, heredity, and antisocial behavior in the minds of both professionals and the general public around the turn of the century had serious consequence in justifying or rationalizing policies of segregation, neglect, and even sterilization of persons considered "genetically unfit" (Whitney and Shick, 1931). Such beliefs justified the growth of institutions in this country. "With concern over the social aspects of retardation, with increasing 'evidence' that the retarded were in large part criminally inclined, potential perverts, and in any case dysgenic and socially dangerous, the only alternative appeared to be to place the retarded in segregated facilities" (Crissey, 1975, p. 803).

Popularized by pedigree studies such as *The Kallikak Family* (Goddard, 1912) and *The Jukes* (Dugdale, 1875; 1877), the idea caught the imagination of the general public. A study by Karp and colleagues (1995) now attributes the behaviors of the Kallikaks to fetal alcohol syndrome.

In more recent times, the term "moral imbecile" was viewed as a pejorative, but the concept was perpetuated in diagnoses of "psychopathic personality," "sociopathic personality," conduct disorder, and other characterological disorders (Cleckley, 1964; American Psychiatric Association, 1994; Kazdin, 1990; Quay, 1986). As the impact of social factors became better understood, genetic etiology was no longer accepted without question, at least not as the sole determinant of such behavior. Yet the concept of an inherited predisposition to antisocial behavior remained with us, still intriguing writers and psychologists. Today, the emerging field of behavioral genetics adds new insights into this nineteenth-century concept. The new technology and theoretical implications of recombinant DNA may well lead to the conclusion that antisocial behavior, long attributed to poor environment or deviant social learning, may have some genetic basis.

The concept of the "moral imbecile" traces back to early conceptions of mental retardation as deriving from a violation of the "natural laws." The label varied but definition of the presumed condition remained constant. Howe (1848) defined "moral idiocy" as:

> That condition in which the sentiments, the conscience, the religious feeling, the love of neighbor, the sense of beauty, . . . are so far dormant or underdeveloped as to incapacitate the person from being a law unto himself, in anything like the degree which is usual with others of his age. This, . . . exist(s) while the intellectual faculties are quite active . . . It appeared to us certain that the evidence of so many idiots in every generation must be the consequence of some violation of the natural laws; that where there was so much suffering, there must have been sin. We resolved, therefore, to seek for the source of the evil, as well as to gauge the depth and extent of the misery. (pp.15-20)

Forty-five years later, Fernald, superintendent of the Massachusetts School for the Feebleminded, showed equal concern:

> This class of moral imbeciles may show little or no deficiency of the intellectual faculties, but in early childhood manifest a marked absence or perversion of the moral sense as shown by motiveless, persistent lying and thieving, a blind and headstrong impulse toward arson, and a delight in cruelty to animals or to young, helpless companions. These children, if they live, are predestined to become inmates of hospitals or jail, and for the good of the community should be early recognized and subjected to life-long moral quarantine. (Fernald, 1893, pp. 11-12)

Isaac Kerlin, superintendent of one of the nation's first schools for mentally retarded people (Pennsylvania), from the end of the American Civil War until his death in 1893, also was alarmed by this class of individuals:

> . . . To constitute a case of moral imbecility we must have badness without reason, violence without motive, deception

without purpose, thieving without acquisitiveness, brutality inspired by a fiendish love of inflicting pain. There may be a clear apprehension of right and wrong, but an inability to choose the right because overborne by the seductiveness and sensationalism of the wrong. (Kerlin, 1889, p. 34)

Kerlin's successor, Martin Barr, who was also a recognized leader in the field, wrote the first American textbook on mental retardation. Barr was an outspoken advocate of segregation, training, and selective sterilization of persons with mental retardation and expressed particular concern over the moral imbecile:

There is a dangerous element in our midst, an element unprotected and unprovided for; this is our heritage from the last century. The safety of society, therefore, demands its speedy recognition and separation in order to arrest a rapid and appalling increase, and furthermore, its permanent detention lest it permeate the whole body socialistic. (Barr, 1904, p. 326)

Barr published a series of case studies of persons he believed exemplified this diagnosis (Barr, 1909; 1911; 1912; 1914):

K.G. Boy: 9 years; reads and writes fairly well; has no moral anchor; a liar, thief, mischief maker; always in trouble; a tramp; could not resist the "wanderlust"; ran away and worked his way on a cattle steamer to Antwerp and back; little known of family, except that they were respectable people, two brothers being Lutheran ministers.

F.H. Boy: 13 years; expression sly and stealthy; tobacco fiend; fond of opium and strong drink; a liar, thief, malicious, cruel, destructive; dangerous with fire; expert at picking locks; discovered a method of opening a six-lever padlock with six pins; in jail three times before eleventh year for thieving and malicious mischief; can read and write a little but as he already uses every mental acquirement only for evil, no effort has been made to equip him further in that direction; a dangerous character; a menace to society, he should always be kept under close custodial care; father a habitual drunkard, insane, and syphilitic was 55; and mother who was subjected to ill treatment during pregnancy at time of birth of child, who was illegitimate. (Barr, 1904, p. 281)

In 1904, Barr argued for a national policy of eugenic sterilization:

Let asexualization be once legalized, not as penalty for crime but a remedial measure preventing crime and tending to the future comfort and happiness of the defective; let the practice once become common for young children immediately upon being adjudged defective by competent authorities properly appointed, and the public mind will accept it as a matter of course in dealing with defectives; and as an effective means of race preservation it will come to be regarded just as is quarantine—simply a protection against ill. (Barr, 1904, p. 191)

Contrary to popular opinion, Dugdale was not a staunch advocate of the hereditary transmission of moral or temperamental qualities, nor did he believe his study of the Jukes supported this contention. In a paper titled "Hereditary Pauperism" (1875), Dugdale acknowledged the success of animal breeders in perpetuating desired temperamental traits in their stocks but indicated that application of this analogy to human beings was unsound:

The human being, having the power to alter his environment, has produced such a variety of changes in that portion of it which relates to his social relations, that no fixedness of moral character could be established which would correspond to the automacy of instinct as found in the insect or the bird . . . As we approach features which are molded by education, they are less transmissible, and more completely governed by the laws of variation, which are largely referable to environment. (p. 82)

Goddard's (1912) Kallikak family study, more than any other single event, created in the popular mind an association between mental retardation and socially deviant behavior. Although Goddard's methodology and conclusions (indeed, even his honesty) have been challenged (Smith, 1985), the disparity in behavior between the two lines of descent of Martin Kallikak offered convincing proof to many in its day, not only that mental retardation was inherited, but also that retardation supplied the seeds of pauperism, crime, and prostitution.

Smith (1985) quotes correspondence from Goddard in 1948 taking exception to being characterized as an hereditarian. Goddard denied any intention of deemphasizing environment "because in those days environment was not being considered. It is not the criminal that is unmodifiable. Much can be done for the criminal and the pauper. It is their inferior brain which they have inherited that cannot be modified . . . " (see Smith, 1985, p. 134).

If Goddard did not espouse the inheritance of behavioral traits, he came remarkably close. In fact, he seemed to vacillate in this belief. He had no doubt that mental retardation was the source of social problems because of both limited intellect and greater fecundity:

> No amount of work in the slums or removing the slums from our cities will ever be successful until we take care of those who make the slums what they are. . . . If all the slum districts of our cities were removed tomorrow and model tenements built in their places, we would still have slums in a week's time because we have those mentally defective people who can never be taught to live otherwise than they have been living. (Goddard, 1912, pp. 70-71)

The association between retardation and crime did not die easily. In Pennsylvania, as late as the 1950s, the superintendent of the state's largest private facility for mentally retarded persons lobbied at state and national levels for sterilization of the "genetically unfit," and sterilizations were performed at this facility for persons who demonstrated unmanageable behaviors (Whitney and Shick, 1931).

By the 1920s, a softening in attitude becomes apparent. Fernald, who did much to promulgate the concept of the moral imbecile, gave voice to this new attitude in his presidential address to the national association of mental retardation superintendents. Acknowledging that the pedigree studies of Goddard and others established that mental retardation is often hereditary, Fernald then described what he termed "the legend of the feebleminded," namely that criminal and antisocial tendencies were a characteristic of people with mental retardation:

> This legend conveyed the impression that the feebleminded were almost all of the highly hereditary class; they were almost invariably immoral, most of the women bore illegitimate children; nearly all were antisocial, vicious and criminal; they were all idle and shiftless and seldom supported themselves; they were highly dangerous people roaming up and down the earth seeing whom they might destroy . . . (p. 221)

> The [legend] was based on a study of the only known large groups of defectives of that period and they were those who *had* got into trouble and *were* in institutions, who *were* largely of the hereditary class and *had* behaved badly and *were* shiftless and lazy . . .
> Since that time many things have happened to make us believe that we have been far too sweeping in some of our generalization and deductions concerning the feebleminded. Entirely new cross-sections of feeblemindedness have been revealed in the study of thousands of unselected mental defectives in special school classes, school clinics, in private practice in school and community surveys, and in the army tests. The after-care studies of discharged inmates of institutions and of graduates of special classes have taught us much about adult feeblemindedness . . . there are thousands of mental defectives where we believed there were hundreds. . . . We must not forget that Goddard not only named the moron but he discovered him (by the use of intelligence testing). The apparent increase in numbers is largely due to the inclusion of these newly discovered morons. The clinical history of many of these pupils suggests that infective, inflammatory or other destructive brain disease in infancy was the cause of mental defect. . . .
> After-care studies of many defectives discharged from institutions, who have no innately vicious character defects and who have been given habits of obedience, and protected from evil companions and taught to work during the formative period of their lives, usually behave well if they are given

continuing, friendly supervision. . . . Much of their bad behavior in the institution probably was the institutional expression which every adolescent exhibits. (Fernald, 1924, pp. 211-213)

## RECOGNITION OF OTHER DETERMINANTS

The recognition of organic determinants of mental retardation was reinforced by the research of Strauss and Lehtinen (1947) who distinguished between exogenous and endogenous causation. Yet, genetic determination of the type of antisocial behavior described by Howe, Fernald, and Barr has never been ruled out. Indeed, there is evidence that genetics does play a role. Contemporary diagnostic classifications of Antisocial Personality, Borderline Personality, and Conduct Disorder appear closest to the moral imbecile described by early workers. Antisocial Personality involves a history of behavioral disorder beginning before the age of fifteen and including crime, violence, and delinquency. Diagnosis of Borderline Personality is made upon evidence of impulsivity, unstable relationships, intense, uncontrolled anger, affective instability, identity disturbance, feelings of boredom, and frantic efforts to avoid real or imagined abandonment (APA, 1994).

The publication of Hunt's *Intelligence and Experience* (1961) did much to persuade psychologists that environmental factors greatly influence the growth of intellect, especially during certain critical periods of development. This notion became especially popular during the Kennedy-Johnson era, since it seemed to further justify through scientific evidence the war on poverty.

The 1960s witnessed the rediscovery of Skeels and Dye's (1939) data on the effects of environmental stimulation in reversing the manifestations of mental retardation. These researchers in the 1930s and 1940s reported significant increments in tested intelligence in children taken from orphanages and foundling homes and placed into more stimulating environments. No such increments were found in children remaining in the homes. Their conclusions, so radically different from prevailing ideas about the irreversibility of mental retardation, were not taken seriously until two decades had gone by. There was a burgeoning of environmental investigations (e.g., Garber, 1988) as well as far-reaching social programs of early education, such as Headstart. The role of social factors in mental retardation was more firmly established by two landmark volumes by Begab, Haywood, and Garber (1981). During this era of unbridled optimism, some scientists believed and fostered the idea that mental retardation eventually would be eliminated by proper methods of social engineering (Wolfensberger, 1971a, 1971b). Genetic factors of etiology were all but forgotten.

Accordingly, social and cognitive psychologists rejected the concept of aggressive personalities possessing a constantly operating aggressive drive, either conscious or unconscious. Instead, they emphasized the role of learning aggressive responses to specific situational cues (Berkowitz, 1962) or the imitation of aggressive models (Bandura, 1964, pp. 274-288; Bandura and Walters, 1959):

> . . . The habitually hostile person is someone who has developed a particular attitude toward large segments of the world about him. He has learned to interpret (or categorize) a wide variety of situations and/or people as threatening or otherwise frustrating to him. Anger is aroused when these interpretations are made, and the presence of relevant cues—stimuli associated with frustrating events—then evoke the aggressive behavior. In many incidents the anger seems to become "short-circuited" with continued repetition of the sequence so that the initial thought responses alone elicit hostile behavior. (Berkowitz, 1962, pp. 258-259)

By the 1960s, these concepts were challenged by a series of studies that reported abnormally high prevalence of males with an extra Y chromosome (XYY) in prisons (Jacobs et al., 1968; Court Brown 1968). Many of these persons had histories of overt aggressive behaviors, crimes of violence, sexual offenses, tallness, and mental subnormality. These findings led some writers to conclude that the additional Y chromosome exerts a powerful influence in the genesis of aggressive behavior (Montagu, 1968). While Montagu denied that the extra Y chromosome necessarily predisposes to aggressive behavior, he felt that it does exert sufficient pressure to justify a program of early screening and "social therapy" to teach behavioral control.

The issue is far from clear, but the higher incidence of antisocial behaviors in persons with XYY chromosome complements has been replicated many times. Price and Whatmore (1967), for example, found no difference in XYY males and control XY males at the same hospital with respect to social deprivation or family history of crime or mental retardation. However, for the XYY males, the onset of behavioral disturbance and the age of first conviction were earlier. XYY males seemed impervious to corrective measures and demonstrated a lack of remorse and a limited capacity for affection and interpersonal relationships. However, not all XYY males are aggressive. The higher incidence of XYY males in prisons does not prove that the extra Y chromosome caused the behavior that led to their incarceration. Such behavior may be dependent on a host of environmental variables (Kessler and Moos, 1969; Baker, 1972).

Edward Zigler, a staunch defender of the importance of genetics, has argued for a balanced two-factor theory of mental retardation (Zigler and Hodapp, 1986). Zigler interprets the bimodal distribution of intelligence (Dingman and Tarjan, 1960) as indicating two types of conditions: (1) the lower end of the normal distribution curve representing people who are primarily mildly retarded variants of a multigenetically determined intellectual level; this category also includes people who are mentally retarded because of social or cultural factors and are not qualitatively different from the general population; and (2) those with organic conditions or specific chromosomal or genetic defects; these persons tend to be moderately to profoundly retarded and appear to be qualitatively different from the general population. Presumably the group of persons with antisocial behaviors being considered here would be drawn from the first group. However, some additional genetic factor would be needed to explain their social deviation on the basis of heredity.

## THE NEW GENETICS

More recent technology based on the understanding of recombinant DNA has led to the identification of specific genetic loci of many medical syndromes. Gene mapping has also proven to be of value in identifying genetic determinants of syndromes associated with mental retardation, many with behavioral manifestations. The genetic literature points to specific behaviors associated with conditions such as Rett Syndrome, Fragile X Syndrome, Williams Syndrome, Smith-Magenis Syndrome, and others. Associated behaviors are usually stereotyped movements such as arm flapping, self-hugging, and gaze avoidance. Even behaviors traditionally understood as psychologically determined are now being linked to genetic factors. Although the research methodology demonstrating their presumed associations has been lacking in sophistication (Rosen, 1993), evidence is growing that many of these behaviors are, indeed, biologically driven. To date, no one has established a genetic locus for antisocial behavior. If there is such a link, would the Y chromosome be a logical place to search? Are other chromosomes involved, as would be necessary to explain genetically determined antisocial behavior in women? What is the role of environmental inputs such as aggressive role models (Bandura and Walters, 1959; Bandura, 1962) and child abuse? (See Chapter 6.) To what extent do cognitive factors operate to control aggressive impulse (Beck et al., 1979; Ellis, 1974; Lazarus, 1976; Meichenbaum, 1977)? The identification of genetic determinants will raise as many questions as it answers.

Early workers were more inclined to include morality in their classification and definitions of deviant behavior than we are today. The first workers with the retarded included moral training as an essential ingredient in the educational curriculum. Current thinking typically ignores moralistic distinctions as too value laden and unscientific. One exception has been in the definition of insanity, tracing back to British law. The M'Naghten rule of insanity (Hagan, 1994, pp. 220-223), used for generations by the courts, has been modified to include not only the ability to tell right from wrong but also the control required to act upon this knowledge. It seems reasonable to include criteria of understanding (cognitive) and control in defining the characteristics of persons labeled as having antisocial personality or conduct disorder. A third defining characteristic is the absence of a sense of remorse. The possibility that genetic factors may determine some or all of these dimensions of functioning remains intriguing. Variations in the relative strengths of these dimensions may account for differences in clinical manifestations. Clever sociopaths may well be aware that what they are doing is what society regards as wrong, and they, themselves, may admit it is wrong. They may also have the resources for personal control. Yet, because of deviant motivational structure, they may develop no feelings of remorse for noncompliance with societal mores. Border-line personalities may have a cognitive awareness of right and wrong and may feel remorse, yet still be unable to control antisocial behavior. Some mentally retarded offenders may be low in all three dimensions.

It is natural to cling to the belief that what is current represents progress and what has gone before is old fashioned and inadequate. Each era brings with it a set of assumptions about the events with which it deals—its own concepts, descriptive language, and convictions of the validity of its constructs and methods. Older workers nod knowingly, recognizing their own shibboleths now garbed in new attire, but willingly hold their tongues and move with the flow of "progress." Examination of the concept of the moral imbecile results in the disquieting revelation that perhaps we have not traveled so far after all. Certainly our language has undergone considerable alteration. The term "imbecile," and similarly its companions "idiot" and "moron," has been abandoned because of pejorative connotations. The word "moral" also tends to make some of us uncomfortable. Distinctions between what is moral or immoral in a changing society create thorny problems for social planners. The teaching of values to behaviorally aberrant adolescents is explored further in Chapter 9. Similarly, the judgmental implications of mental retardation representing divine retribution for violation of "natural laws" has long been discarded. Intemperance, sloth, adultery, incest, and other excesses have lost some of their taint. Modern knowledge of etiology precludes consideration of "sins of the fathers" as causative or predisposing mechanisms. Yet, the conviction of nineteenth-century writers that mental retardation is hereditary returns, and who can deny that fetal alcohol syndrome and "crack" are the contemporary equivalents of natural law violations?

Modern technology that includes the unlocking of mysteries through gene mapping; the possibility of gene alteration by gene splicing, compensatory metabolic changes, and chemical intervention at the synaptic level (see Chapter 11), and advances in our understanding of social and environmental factors all portend improved treatment, prevention, and control of social deviance.

# Chapter 5

# Agents of Change

"The key to treatment rests with the direct care staff. I wish we knew how to keep people motivated and trained."

"I would think that after all these years of providing services you would have solved that problem."

"It never changes. Salary levels remain low. Staff turnover is always a problem. It is difficult to keep staff motivated. Many start out enthusiastic and eager to provide treatment. But they burn out easily. Longtime workers exert pressure upon those who are too 'gung ho.' Some staff scream at residents and harass them. They respond to confrontations by becoming angry and defensive rather than trying to determine the reason for the child's behavior. Yet not always. Just recently a direct care worker was confronted by a child having a severe tantrum. Instead of merely handling the child physically, he asked what had set him off. The boy, who was especially hairy, was being taunted with the label 'wolfman' by the other children. The worker arranged for the child to have his hair cut and a shave. It made a big difference. Another worker reacted to a general uprising of several aggressive males by starting to sing and clap his hands. The boys joined in with the singing and clapping and the incident was over. But those incidents are probably the exception. Weekends are difficult. It's hard to provide programs for children all day long. No wonder they find ways to make trouble. Often they're bored."

"Raise salaries."

"It doesn't always solve the problem."

"Provide better supervision."

"We do until there is a budget crunch."

"Training?"

"It helps. We're improving."

## THE DIRECT CARE POSITION

Until the early 1960s, cottage parents at residential facilities were usually women. Their official designation was "Matron," although they were often called "Mom" by the residents. Since many of the children were orphaned or abandoned by their natural parents, the maternal designation was not regarded as inappropriate. Matrons usually advanced up the ranks, starting as attendants until they became unit managers. In this role as manager they had a great deal of authority. They ruled with an iron fist and meted out discipline to residents and staff alike. Very little training was provided, and few of the women who filled these positions had any formal background in child development, psychology, or management. Generally, however, they ran a tight ship. With the advent of a more modern rehabilitation program, the position of Matron changed. It was recognized that males as well as females were necessary to serve as role models for children. Greater attempts at providing in-service training were made, but the position remained low status and low paying, and generally, the staff were undereducated for their roles.

The cottage parents described at "Hollymeade" by Polsky (1962) were older persons in search of security and attached to children. They were not upwardly mobile within the institution and had very limited participation in the treatment team. As mentioned in Chapter 1, they walked a very narrow line in attempting to accommodate to the delinquent culture of the cottage.

The delivery of residential services to persons with mental or emotional disabilities relies heavily upon the competence and motivation of direct care staff. There can be little argument that the direct care worker is the backbone of any residential program. A survey of mental health facilities in the United States (Manderscheid and Sonnenschein, 1992) reports that in 1988, 71 percent of the staff of such facilities, over 381,000 people, were in patient care positions. Yet, it is generally acknowledged that direct care workers are underpaid, have relatively low status, have inadequate training (Zlomke and Benjamin, 1983), have insufficient knowledge of handicapping conditions (Scheerenberger, 1970; Slater and Bunyard, 1983), experience high rates of burnout and turnover (Lakin et al., 1982), and are often chronically frustrated and dissatisfied with their jobs (Cleland and

Peck, 1967; Thaw and Wolfe, 1986). Despite widespread efforts to upgrade the position, the job category remains unpopular and presents constant recruitment challenges. It is not surprising that little therapeutic intervention takes place in many residential treatment units.

Staff who provide the direct care of the children in residential treatment facilities may represent the greatest challenge to RTF administrators and clinicians. They are the true treatment agents since they have the most immediate and most direct contact with the children. It is this cadre of staff that translates the therapeutic goals of psychologists, psychiatrists, and social workers into action. These are the people who must be relied upon to create the therapeutic milieu. It is they who must enforce the climate of safety. They become the substitute parents and family while the child is in placement. They are the ones who will be present evenings and weekends and holidays and during third shift if the child awakens with a nightmare. They must parent, protect, nurture, and treat. They are the role models against which the child may measure him- or herself— the heroes he or she should emulate.

How successful is the RTF in attracting, selecting, and training people to meet these standards? Do persons drawn to the child care profession demonstrate the cognitive, emotional, and motivational attributes necessary to perform their jobs? Do they have the moral qualities with which we would like children to identify? Such data are not available. What has been studied extensively are the attitudes of direct care workers in hospitals, institutions, and correctional facilities for children.

Direct care workers often represent the least educated, lowest paid, and most poorly trained segment of the residential facility. They often represent an economically disadvantaged segment of society. Numerous surveys have documented that this group views itself as unappreciated by management. Their job satisfaction is low; their turnover rate high. They spend the overwhelming portion of each workday in maintenance and custodial activities rather than in teaching or counseling residents. In an RTF for emotionally disturbed children, they bear the burden of discipline and control so that, unfortunately, the role of guard or jailer becomes implicit in their jobs. They do not see themselves as having the necessary skills to influence children or change the children's behavior. Often they choose a health service occupation because few other options exist for them and will leave if a more lucrative opportunity arises (Rice and Rosen, 1991; Rice, Rosen, and Macmann, 1991). Yet, many direct care workers begin their jobs with optimism and enthusiasm. They appear to suffer a high degree of stress in many instances, and the rate of burnout may be higher than in comparable paying, nonhuman service fields.

In most treatment settings, there exist two distinct levels of staff. The direct care staff, representing the lowest rung of the status hierarchy, serve to maintain staff-to-child ratios imposed by regulatory agencies. The so-called professional treatment team of psychologists, psychiatrists, social workers, case managers, program supervisors, and administrators who direct the treatment efforts are predominantly white. Relationships between the two groups are often strained. Clinicians complain about the residential staff for their poor attitudes, rough handling of children, failure to follow through on treatment plans, failure to document incidents and progress accurately, and sometimes, abuse of children. Direct care staff complain that clinicians have little understanding of the children since they are not present during most of the day and that they have book knowledge and degrees but little practical, hands-on competence in handling crises and emergencies. Direct care staff also resent that, as first-line workers, they are constantly exposed to situations that may make them liable for abuse charges by children, some of whom learn to use such charges as a means of revenge against staff.

## *TRAINING*

Despite these harsh realities, the situation is not hopeless. Technologies exist with proven effectiveness in modifying inappropriate behavior, and the direct care staff are the logical implementers of such technology. This is an area they can identify as their own and use as a career builder. Likewise, we have elegant and useful personality theories and strategies for dealing with depression, elevating self-esteem, increasing self-efficacy of disadvantaged children, and helping them overcome feelings of helplessness. The greater accessibility of the children to the direct care worker, and often their greater familiarity with the culture from which the children derive, really does make the workers potentially powerful as agents of change.

At one RTF, direct care staff are accepted as essential and contributing members of the treatment team. A training curriculum has been developed that begins with two weeks of instruction before staff start to work in the program and continues at regular intervals each year. At least forty hours of instruction are provided annually. The curriculum includes such areas as crisis intervention; fire and safety; CPR; effective parenting; diagnostic entities; psychological testing; the history of child welfare in this country; treatment models; psychotropic medication; behavior management; dealing with sexuality issues; the impact of physical and sexual abuse; attachment, separation, and loss; child development; discipline and motivation; structuring positive interactions; and principles of counseling. Seasoned direct care workers are also included in the orientation of new employees so that new staff may have an opportunity to ask questions and receive realistic accounts of the task requirements.

One important component of training is a set of recommendations about managing critical situations in which staff are confronted with aggressive behavior. With seasoned staff, a slightly different approach to training is used. Staff are asked to become partners in formulating the procedures to be followed rather than asking them to accept an established and irreversible methodology. The trainer acknowledges that administrators are not always in the best position to judge the feasibility of approaches that make good textbook sense. The reactions and contributions of staff are sought and are found to be insightful and helpful. If staff suggest an approach that is negative or psychologically unsound, the trainer explains why it cannot be accepted, and the group works on another approach. This approach to training and program development not only enhances the effectiveness of the treatment interventions with residents but also improves morale and makes for a smoother operating, more cohesive treatment team. The selection, training, and cultivation of competent direct care staff should be accepted as the highest priority in developing effective residential treatment for children. Direct care workers deserve recognition, training, status, and involvement in the treatment process, including decision making about children. This is more than a matter of entitlement; it is essential for residential treatment to work. Child care workers must behave in very specific ways, even when children are being negative, defiant, challenging, and provocative. The following are principles we encourage staff to adhere to:

- Don't become physical with a child unless he or she is endangering him or herself or others and then only by approved methods.
- Let the child know when you are pleased by a behavior and when you are disappointed.
- Be accepting of the child's cultural background. However, do not be reluctant to expose the child to alternative behaviors if they will work better.
- Don't be seduced into accepting a challenge from a child.
- If you become angry at a child who needs attention for negative behavior, you may have temporarily lost your effectiveness. Walk away and allow another worker to intervene.
- Be satisfied with slow, steady progress. Don't be discouraged by setbacks. Learning is not a straight-line function. Bear in mind the reason that the child is in residential placement.
- Never compromise the child's self-esteem. If possible, allow the child to save face.
- Treat families with respect, even if you know that the family has been dysfunctional or even abusive.
- When a child becomes violent, it may be better to remove others from the scene rather than attempting to remove the child. Become an expert at "talking a child down." A team approach with one person replacing another can be effective.
- Discount the thought, "I'm going to teach this child a lesson." No one can reverse behavioral disorders with one intervention.
- Relationships that you form with children will be more powerful than any intervention you might apply.
- Look beyond the behavior. What is the child expressing by the behavior? These children often have genuine deficits in processing and expression. They tend to communicate by action rather than words.
- Try to get the child to say what is bothering him or her when he or she appears depressed, angry, or afraid. Learn to short-circuit more severe behavior outbursts.
- The worst time to deal with a problem is when the child is out of control. Try to defuse the anger and wait until the child is calm to deal with the underlying problem.

- Use phrases such as "I like the way you did that."; "How can we solve this problem?"; "When you feel better let's talk about it."; "Why don't you go to your room until you calm down and then we'll discuss it?"
- We have found, paradoxically, that very often the staff who are being most negative (e.g., yelling) with the child are those who care the most. They are behaving as they behave toward their own children. The worst staff are less visible due to their indifference.

\* \* \*

The group waited for me to begin. Subdued, anticipating two weeks of training, but unsure of what would be presented, they introduced themselves to each other. They represented mixed backgrounds. Some were fresh out of school—psychology, social work, sociology, and special education majors. Others were transfers from other programs within the RTF or from other treatment facilities. More work hardened, they had been exposed to training before and were somewhat inured to it and skeptical that the aging, professorial-looking trainer would have anything useful to say to them.

I was enjoying the opportunity to interface with them, although the training had torn a massive chunk out of my work schedule. Staff frequently arrive motivated and enthusiastic about the opportunity to work with disturbed children, but after a few weeks of the challenges presented by the children, the paperwork demanded by program managers, and the negative influence of disgruntled veterans of the program, they settle into a routinized apathy and pessimism. Here was an opportunity to prepare them for their assignment and to build a cadre of people with a common knowledge base. Hopefully this type of beginning would sensitize them to the needs of the children, immunize them somewhat against the disappointments, and provide them with the basis of a continuing working partnership.

I had accepted a healthy part of the curriculum as my responsibility. Over the two-week period, I presented a general background about social welfare programs in this country, the backgrounds of the children, the diagnostic process and the most typical diagnostic categories referred to the program, the general principles of behavior modification, an overview of the goals and approaches of counseling, and suggestions for creating a therapeutic milieu. Some of my colleagues presented material covering the various community systems serving children, the involvement of families in counseling and therapy, the educational needs of the children, the admission process, and the various regulations governing program operations, including the numerous record-keeping responsibilities they would need to perform. Instruction in basic first aid skills, crisis intervention techniques, and fire and safety procedures was also provided.

I found the group stimulating. The newly graduated workers were familiar with many of the psychological concepts I presented. They were back in the classroom and eager to show off their book learning. I called upon the more seasoned people to describe their experiences in performing their jobs as caretakers, counselors, and teachers. Some had worked in the juvenile justice system and were exposed to more drastic procedures than we were allowed or motivated to impose. I felt good about the training experience and wondered if we had been successful in hooking them into a cooperative relationship with us. How many would remain in their positions beyond the summer months when more lucrative opportunities beckoned? And would we be able to maintain regular training opportunities to keep the process alive?

## NEW CONCEPTS

The traditional treatment model of RTFs in this country accepts a medical orientation of diagnosis and intervention controlled by professional staff—psychiatrists, psychologists, social workers, and physicians. Aberrant behaviors by the resident population are seen as pathological. Direct care staff and even teachers, while technically a part of the treatment team, are expected to implement treatment plans but not formulate them. Brendtro (1980) has been critical of this approach, offering a "teaching competence" rather than "curing illness" approach as an alternative. This approach is embodied in a movement that has been labeled the "educateur" (educator), originating in Europe and Canada (Daly, 1985). The educateur is a child care worker, trained at the undergraduate or graduate level, responsible for the programming and service delivery in the education and treatment of disturbed children. The position developed in France after World War II when many displaced children required help, exceeding the capabilities of the country's mental health system. The educateur combined the skills of teachers, social workers, psychologists, and recreational activity directors. Training programs and government certification procedures were established. Educateurs functioned in a wide variety of settings including placement centers for mentally retarded, physically handicapped, and emotionally disturbed youngsters. The movement spread to Scotland, Quebec, and later, the United States (Hobbs, 1982, 1983).

At this writing, over a decade later, the educateur concept has not been widely adopted for RTFs. The wide discrepancy between goals, aspirations, morale, status, upward mobility, pay incentives, and effectiveness of professional and so-called paraprofessionals working in treatment centers cries out for a rediscovery of such a concept in order to develop treatment programs to their highest level. The advent of managed care is requiring cheaper, more effective approaches and may well result in such a model.

Shealy (1995) presents a "therapeutic parent" model for the selection and training of children and youth care workers. Reviewing the psychological literature, he finds that the characteristics differentiating good from poor therapists are also those that experts identify as differentiating the best and the worst child and youth care workers. Experts give highest priority to "doing no harm" in elaborating the characteristics of the best workers. Harm derives from situations in which the workers mirror the same negative characteristics of the natural parents (abusiveness, proneness to anger/explosiveness, pathology, and dishonesty) that also characterized the pathology of the parents. Out-of-home care is not necessarily better or worse than care in the home. The critical issue is whether the worker can establish a strong and stable emotional bond with a specific child or youth.

Personal characteristics of good workers include such attributes as flexibility, maturity, common sense, appropriate values, responsibility, a positive self-image, and self-control. The work behaviors of the best child care workers should include the provision of counseling. Their knowledge and skill level should include human development, psychopathology, and treatment options. These standards provide a goal not yet attained at most RTFs.

# Chapter 6

# Adolescence, Violence, and Abuse

"Have you any idea what abuse does to kids?"

"I have no personal experience. We both come from families in which that idea was unthinkable, although my old man did not hesitate to wallop me if he thought I deserved it. It made me angry, but I never considered it abuse."

"The situations we hear about go a lot further than physical punishment for transgressions."

"OK, but are they real?"

"Do you mean false memory syndrome?"

"Exactly. Naive and overly zealous therapists inadvertently planting an idea of abuse. Clients are motivated to please the therapist. Memory is sometimes a flimsy rope with which to hang a parent for something that may or may not have happened a long time ago."

"I agree. There was a good review of the topic by Loftus in the *American Psychologist* a few years back. I know all the allegations are not true. We have our share of false allegations in the program. A worker leans hard on a child for his behavior and the child gets back at him. Remember, these are angry, streetwise kids who know how to survive in settings a lot tougher than the RTF. But abuse does occur. There are mechanisms for investigating charges. Some of our children have fathers in prison because of these charges. Someone has decided they were real. The impact may be devastating. I have been a therapist for many years, but the first time I witnessed a true 'flashback'—a dissociative reaction—it was sobering."

\* \* \*

Billy wakes up each morning thrashing and crying, "No Dad, no Dad!" He and his sister were abused sexually until their mom found out. Now she is remarried and Billy is at the RTF. Billy set fires and became violently aggressive at home and in school. Two prior psychiatric hospitalizations had little effect. He was well-behaved in the hospital and was discharged.

## ADOLESCENT PSYCHOPATHOLOGY: A DEVELOPMENTAL PERSPECTIVE

Pathology in adolescence can be understood as part of a developmental sequence. It represents a continuation of childhood conflicts and neuroses and a reaction to the stresses of progression to the next developmental phase. The impact of social factors such as violence, trauma, and abuse add an understanding of what it is that the child is struggling to cope with. However, sociological analysis alone is insufficient to account for the personal meanings of the child's behavior. This chapter provides a basis for understanding the disturbed adolescent against the yardstick of normal adolescent experience and in the context of additional and extraordinary stresses in the form of abuse, neglect, abandonment, poverty, and trauma for a child welfare adolescent in placement. Clinicians accept the premise that behavioral and emotional disturbance in such children can be viewed as a defensive process of the child attempting to master these stresses and to survive.

### Normal Adolescence

Adolescence is ordinarily a time of turmoil with growing importance of peer relations and diminishing importance, at least temporarily, of parents and their values (Shapiro, 1973). As with all stages of development, physical changes of the body and changing demands of the environment create a disequilibrium of the personality. This disharmony is manifested in the form of perceived internal conflict and a search for solutions. It is in these solutions that we look for what we label as pathology in adolescence. It is the work of adolescence to master the physiological changes that occur as well the changes in the sense of self that accompany greater needs for autonomy and independence and achievement of a sense of identity.

The emergence of secondary sexual characteristics creates anxiety concerning whether development will occur, and will the product that develops be adequate. Although this is particularly evident when physical development is somewhat delayed, feelings of personal inadequacy occur in all early adolescents. Conflicts that were unresolved in early childhood become reactivated and intensified with the surge of libido associated with puberty. The adolescent is particularly vulnerable to assaults upon his competence. Feelings of inferiority are easily aroused, and acceptance by peers replaces acceptance by parents and family as the highest priority. Concerns about the body may border on the hypochondriacal. "Whether it be muscular size or strength, acne, hair, weight, the same general pattern of anxiety prevails. Is it working right? Is it normal? Can I control it? These patterns are most often clearly delineated in the young adolescent's struggles with masturbation" (Shapiro, 1973, p. 98).

Intertwined with the need for mastery is that for independence. This requires a restructuring of object relationships, namely a rebellion against parental attachments and values. Adolescent boys may become dirty and messy, reminiscent of the behavior of the two-year-old. Outrageous behaviors appear designed to irritate parents and other authority figures and to gain acceptance of peers. The desire to "make the team" or be "one of the gang" replaces meeting parental expectations for scholastic excellence. Adolescent rebellion is also seen by some as motivated by the need to deny sexual feelings toward the opposite-sex parent. This transition is drastic and does not occur smoothly. It is accompanied by extreme mood fluctuations and often signs of depression. The adolescent's self-centeredness and his or her sense of urgency about his or her own needs may be defensive mechanisms designed to ward off feelings of depression. Adolescents may identify with groups that they perceive as oppressed or disadvantaged. This newfound social awareness may be part of the general estrangement from their parents who are seen as representing the establishment. Involvement with drugs is also an expression of rebellion and a need for peer acceptance.

Do these generalizations hold also for children being served at RTFs? Probably more so. When parents fail as role models, when they are unable to provide the luxuries provided routinely to middle-class children, when they are violent or abusive or incapacitated by drugs, then it is likely easier to rebel against them. Adolescent rebellion in such cases may come earlier, last longer, and be of greater intensity. Involvement with peers may be even more intense since such acceptance does more than replace parental attachment; it may substitute for what was never there. When families are dysfunctional and children have never formed stable attachments, the gang may substitute for the family so that the child develops a sense of loyalty that surpasses societal norms in influencing behavior. Attachment disorders have been observed in ADHD children as well as those with fetal alcohol syndrome. It may be that the failure of a child to form normal attachments to their families, for either biological or environmental reasons, makes the child more susceptible to peer influence. Without a counteracting influence, peer pressures from a gang subculture assume enormous power.

Given the insecurity of adolescence, the rebellion born of drives toward independence, as well as the absence of stable, responsible, adult role models, the pull toward antisocial behavior may be difficult to resist. It is upon this stage that histories of violence and abuse play out their roles.

## *EFFECTS OF VIOLENCE*

Children who grow up in areas where the frequency of violence and crime are high have a high likelihood of being witness to violence. Marans and Cohen (1993) report that 40 percent of sixth-, eighth-, and tenth-graders in New Haven in 1992 reported witnessing at least one violent crime in the past year. Pynoos and Eth (1985) estimated that children witness approximately 10 to 20 percent of the homicides committed in Los Angeles. Bell and Jenkins (1991) report that one-third of African-American children in a Chicago inner-city neighborhood had witnessed a homicide, and two-thirds had witnessed a serious assault. Other studies made it clear that such frightening statistics are not limited to adolescents but are typical of younger children as well. Even worse, children are also victims of crime. Fifty-one percent of New Orleans fifth-graders and 32 percent of Washington, DC, children have been victims of violence (Osofsky, 1995). Although the long-term impact of such events requires further study, there is already increasing evidence that consequences may be serious. Associations between exposure to violence in young children and post-traumatic symptoms and disorders have been reported (Drell, Siegel, and Gaensbaur, 1993; Zeanah, 1994).

Osofsky reports three types of reactions: (1) the development of aggressive behavior and negative emotions; (2) post-traumatic stress disorder; and (3) early relationship problems. Exposure to violence may result in difficulties in children differentiating among emotional states and in being able to give adequate verbal expression of feelings (Pynoos, 1993). Self-attributions of blame, ineffectiveness, and shame may result. The end result may be similar to consequences of abuse and neglect.

School-age children exposed to violence may develop increased anxiety, sleep disturbances, attention difficulties, and intrusive thoughts. Stressors in life may result in flashbacks and reexperiencing the traumatic event, avoidance reactions, and psychological numbing of responsiveness or even overarousal (Osofsky, 1995).

Exposure to violence and trauma may decrease the child's capacity to trust and form relationships with others. Furthermore, parents become more protective and may interfere with the development of autonomy and independence in their children as a means of protecting them.

Treatment of these reactions must first establish the current safety of the child—no small order in inner-city slum areas. It is significant that some children do build up a resilience to violence that seems to occur more frequently when there is a safe haven and when parents or others are viewed as supportive and protective. Individual intellectual or temperamental traits may also serve to help the children learn ways of coping with violence.

An ecological, developmental model describing how children learn to become violent has been described by Fraser (1996). Noting that assaultive behavior tends to occur in families across generations and that a small percentage of families account for a disproportionate amount of violence, the author addresses factors that may account for the learning of this behavior. Generally, the model depicts violent behavior in children as the "result of impoverished opportunity structures and inadequate training in social and cognitive skills, perception that there is social and concrete utility in aggressive behavior, and lack of indigenous rewards for prosocial activity in the social environment" (p. 349). Drawing heavily upon research findings (Patterson, DeBaryshe, and Ramsey, 1989; Reid and Patterson, 1989; Patterson, Capaldi, and Bank, 1991), Fraser distinguishes between "early starter" and "late starter" models, referring to whether aggressive patterns begin in early childhood or early adolescence.

In early onset situations, children are trained by families to respond to authority with hostility by using harsh punishment, a failure to set consistent limits, neglect in rewarding prosocial behavior, and a coercive style of parent-child interactions. Parents are inconsistent in their response to oppositional behavior, either failing to provide intervention or responding with excessive force and negative affect. Children fail to learn adequate problem-solving skills, such as negotiation, from their parents and may also learn that aggressive behavior pays off. Early aggressiveness is associated with more serious aggression and conflict with authority in later years. Aggression in the home situation generalizes to the school and the community. Children who learn violent behaviors at home tend to be rejected in school for nondefensive displays of violence. This increases their sense of isolation and may intensify aggressive behavior. Children who are "late starters" for aggression are more prone to be affected by influences outside the family such as failure in school and neighborhood gangs.

## EFFECTS OF ABUSE

Sexual and physical abuse can be devastating to the mental health of children. Numerous reports exist documenting heightened degrees of aggressiveness (Walker, Bonner, and Kaufman, 1988), anxiety and phobias (Gelinas, 1983), interpersonal difficulties (Courtois, 1979; Herman, 1981), sexual problems (Silbert and Pines, 1981; Steele and Alexander, 1981), suicidal tendencies (Bagley and King, 1990), and depression (Galdston, 1965; Green, 1978) in abused children.

Miller (1993) surveyed eighty-two adolescents with behavioral disorder and seventy adolescents without disabilities on the prevalence, frequency, and conditions associated with sexual and physical abuse among these adolescents. Sexual abuse was highest among females with behavioral disturbances. A similar finding held for the frequency of physical abuse. Even nondisabled females revealed an alarming degree of sexual abuse. Young males in both groups reported more physical abuse than their female counterparts. If these data are representative of larger, behaviorally disturbed populations, it is clear that treatment programs will need to make this problem an important component of their efforts.

## *Effects of Sexual Abuse*

There does not appear to be a general profile of children who have been sexually abused (Kendall-Tackett, Williams, and Finkelhor, 1993). However, certain behaviors occur more frequently. These include heightened levels of fear and anxiety; hyperalertness and hypervigilance; symptoms similar to post-traumatic stress disorder, such as bed-wetting and insomnia; depression, withdrawal, and flattened affect; aggressive sexual behaviors; aggression; property destruction; problems in self-esteem; problems in forming close attachments with others; problems in forming a healthy identity, including the attainment of feelings of significance, virtue, mastery, power, and a sense of being in control.

There are also reported gender differences (Friedrich, 1995), with males more likely than females to develop externalizing patterns such as aggression. As in post-traumatic stress disorder, therapists observe a greater likelihood of dissociating reaction in children who have been abused, i.e., a tendency to compartmentalize or segregate information, experiences, and memories rather than to integrate these aspects into conscious awareness. This mechanism may produce a psychogenic amnesia for the traumatic events. Some children experience flashbacks to the trauma in the form of nightmares or night terror.

## *Fetal Alcohol Syndrome*

The deleterious effects of alcohol upon the fetus have been known since biblical times, although early references placed most of the blame upon drinking by the father. The impacts of fetal exposure to alcohol have been well documented (see Abel, 1984, for an early review of the literature). Generally, drinking during pregnancy may result in spontaneous abortion, premature birth, low birth weight, impaired intrauterine growth rate, and neonatal death. Long-term effects include head and facial abnormalities as well as cardiac defects and disorders of other bodily organs. Disorders of the central nervous system such as mental retardation, other cognitive deficits, developmental delays in maturation and motor development, and behavioral problems such as hyperactivity, impulsivity, and difficulties in concentration have been well recognized for many years.

Animal studies reveal many types of learning disabilities in animals exposed to alcohol in utero, as compared with control animals that were not exposed. There is also some evidence of neuropathological anomalies of the brain in animals exposed to alcohol that were later sacrificed and autopsied.

Inclusion of fetal alcohol syndrome in the present chapter was based on the assertion of some that drinking by a pregnant mother may constitute prenatal child abuse if the drinking endangers the child's health. Abel (1984) reports a case tried in Ontario, Canada, in 1981, in which a mother was successfully prosecuted for violating her unborn child's rights by drinking during pregnancy. The mother, who was an habitual drinker, had already had one child diagnosed with fetal alcohol syndrome. The mother refused to listen to her physician who advised her to stop drinking, and when she continued to drink, he reported her to the local Children's Aid Society. The child, born while the mother was intoxicated, was taken from the mother because of her drinking, which was viewed by the court as physical abuse. The same issues arise now with mothers addicted to crack cocaine and other drugs.

## TREATMENT

It is no revelation that thirteen- and fourteen-year-old children are sexually oriented. The onslaught of puberty, both formidable and daunting to children with less violent backgrounds than those in RTFs, adds gasoline to an already smoldering fire that may quickly erupt into a major conflagration. Place a group of emotionally disturbed adolescents together in an unnatural group-living situation, particularly a coeducational setting, and there is going to be trouble. If these are streetwise children, if they have access to the same movie and television influences as everyone else in our culture, if they are supervised by staff with confused or ambivalent attitudes toward sexuality, incidents and crises are bound to occur.

When there is an inequity in ability levels, power, and dominance among the children who are exposed to each other, these confrontations may be severe, even to the degree of criminality. When the children also have a history of sexual, physical, or emotional abuse, these behaviors may be far more than normal adolescent exploration; rather, they may represent an enactment of traumas and conflicts central to the child's personality. Response to these incidents, which tends, even in the most therapeutically oriented treatment centers, to be disciplinary, may require a degree of treatment sophistication that is rare or nonexistent.

The goals of psychotherapy for abused children center around these symptoms and behaviors. A reparative process requires a safe environment in which the child realizes that the traumas of his or her past will not recur. Within this environment, the child must learn again to trust others, to regain a sense of power and control, to gain some understanding of the trauma, to learn useful coping skills for dealing with pre- and posttrauma issues, and to achieve a realistic sense of optimism about the future. These goals make good sense. Whether they can be accomplished in practice and within the context of a group residential setting is questionable.

The choice of therapy will depend largely upon the setting, the availability of trained staff, the particular theoretical persuasion of the therapist, and funding and political considerations. One approach that has some demonstrated success is that of play therapy (Gil, 1991; 1996; Gil and Johnson, 1993; O'Connor, 1991). Play is a natural technique to use with children, especially those who have experienced abuse, since it does not require a great deal of verbal skill from the child, nor is interpretation a necessary part of the therapeutic process. The play itself is the therapy.

Play therapy is an attempt to relieve the emotional distress of the child through a variety of imaginative and expressive play materials. Puppets, dolls, clay, art, miniature toys, and sand may be used for evaluation and treatment. Through such a medium, the child finds a way to relive traumatic experiences and to resolve issues previously unaddressed. The traditional components of therapy, such as the transference relationship, continue to exist while creative techniques such as storytelling and the use of metaphors may be unique to the approach. The child must be able to answer such questions as "Why did this happen to me?" and "Am I safe now?" An equally important question, especially within the context of the residential treatment center, is "Do I have to become the perpetrator in order to survive?" There is no evidence to suggest that play therapy or any specific theoretical approach is superior to other therapies. In each approach, the sensitivity and skill of the therapist may be paramount.

There are very few published studies, especially of those with control groups, documenting the effectiveness of therapies for sexually abused children. Cognitive therapy is reported by Deblinger, McLeer, and Henry (1989) to have been used successfully with nineteen sexually abused girls diagnosed with post-traumatic stress disorder. Symptoms were relatively stable for several weeks until treatment was initiated. After twelve sessions of therapy, PTSD symptoms were significantly less than before treatment. An interesting study by Lanktree and Briere (1995) reports on the effectiveness of a specific abuse treatment approach used for at least three months with 105 sexually abused children, aged eight to fifteen.

A Trauma Symptom Checklist for Children and a Children's Depression Inventory were administered at three-month intervals. Most traumatic symptoms showed decreases beginning at three months of treatment and continued to decrease. Those still in treatment after one year showed a decrease in anxiety, depression, and posttraumatic stress. Sexual concerns did not show decreases until six months of treatment. Although a comparison group was not studied, multiple regression analyses showed that the amount of time from the end of abuse until either the beginning or end of treatment was far less predictive of symptom reduction than the number of months spent in treatment. Lanktree and Briere interpret this finding as indicating the effects were specific to the treatment rather than merely to the passage of time. Short-term group treatment of sexually abused children has been reported effective in several studies (Friedrich et al., 1992; Heibert-Murphy, deLuca, and Runtz, 1992; McGain and McKinzey, 1995).

# Chapter 7

# Treating Childhood
# Emotional Disorders

"Despite the impact of possible genetic inputs, I still put faith in the counseling and psychotherapy we do, especially the family therapy."

"The old talking cure."

"Don't be so cynical. Outcome studies are generally positive in documenting effective results of psychotherapy."

"You've done such studies with your kids, your therapies?"

"No, I don't know the effectiveness of my own therapy, let alone that of the other therapists."

"Well, you're no worse than most clinicians trusting their interventions without empirical evidence."

"Look, we take kids that come from dysfunctional families with backgrounds of deprivation, neglect, or worse, who are removed from their families and shunted from placement to placement; we give them an opportunity to communicate their feelings, perhaps form a trusting relationship with a helping adult, at least for a while, and maybe even teach them some skills such as handling anger. We keep the therapies practical—day-to-day coping. Perhaps they find some role models with whom to identify. Perhaps they learn that they have options in life—that they have choices. Sure, I can't provide data about outcomes. If they go back to the same squalor and abuse and screw up again, have we failed? There are no guarantees here. Our staff does their best for the most part. They like the kids. Is that so bad?"

\*   \*   \*

About 1 percent of all school children and 6 to 8 percent of all students with handicaps are classified as seriously emotionally disturbed (Gadow, 1986). Although some childhood problems may disappear on their own, early signs of dysfunction such as unmanageability, aggression, and social withdrawal indicate increased risk for serious psychiatric problems in adulthood.

## EARLY APPROACHES

Prior to the nineteenth century, there are few references in the psychological and psychiatric literature pertaining to the treatment of emotional disorders in children. Children were regarded as miniature and imperfect adults rather than as individuals with unique personalities. Aberrant behaviors were regarded as disciplinary problems, with the father as the disciplinarian and his authority coming from the Church. Stone (1974) attributes a turning point to the publication of the *Wild Boy of Aveyron* in 1806 by Jean-Marc-Gaspard Itard, a French physician. This work was an account of the attempt to educate Victor, an unsocialized, probably mentally retarded child found wandering in a wooded area near Paris.

Itard's efforts laid the groundwork for contemporary special education but, to Itard's dismay, did not make the child normal nor even teach him to speak. Itard's work, however, showed a sensitivity to the emotional and social development of the child that was rare for its day. Itard saw in Victor an opportunity to demonstrate the validity of principles of British and French associationism, viewing him as Rousseau's (1754) "noble savage" and Locke's (1804) "tabula rasa." His desire to correct deficits through scientifically determined methods of remediation was a giant leap forward in conceptualization of the needs of deviant children.

A second milestone in the development of a humanistic attitude toward child treatment is attributed to French healer—Franz Anton Mesmer (1779) and his disciples (Stone, 1974). Borrowing heavily from the writings of Richard Meade about magnetic forces and the relationships among heavenly bodies, Mesmer developed a theoretical and practical approach to psychological disorders. His treatment method, which he labeled "animal magnetism," became the vogue in Paris at the close of the century, linking the humanism of Rousseau with the more materialistic conception of the universe as governed by natural forces. Mesmer assumed that men as well as planets influenced each other by setting animal-magnetic fluid in motion. This concept, the forerunner of contemporary concepts of empathy, sympathy, and suggestion, led Freud to the development of psychoanalytic theory and technique. As Stone points out, Freud originally conceived of id, ego, and superego as compartments of the psyche, affording them almost tangible properties of the central nervous system. Despite its materialistic underpinnings, Mesmerism brought child psychiatry a giant step forward because of its humanistic approach to children and its use of psychological treatment modalities.

The origins of psychoanalysis in the clinics and consulting rooms of Vienna are well known and need not be extensively elaborated here. Most noteworthy was the innovative focus upon the importance of childhood as the bedrock of adult neuroses and the elaboration of the theory of the instincts exerting their force from birth in determining childhood sexuality and psychosexual development. Children were worthy of treatment, not only to help them through childhood but also to prevent adult manifestations of sexuality. It is also significant that adults were brought into treatment, sharing in the responsibility for children's symptoms because of overly harsh or overly lenient child-rearing practices.

While child psychiatry was burgeoning at the beginning of this century, academic psychology was still largely preoccupied with nomothetic, empirical approaches to studying sensation, perception, and learning. General laws of behavior were the primary concern, with individual differences considered to be experimental error. Clinical treatment and psychopathology were considered outside the realm of the academic establishment.

The twentieth century brought a new focus on the individual (Allport, 1961), the application of learning theory to practical problems of child training (Watson, 1924), and the evaluation and treatment of development and emotional problems in the psychological clinic (Witmer, 1896).

Watson, known today as the father of American behaviorism, involved himself in all aspects of child development and was viewed as an expert by the media. Describing behavior in stimulus-response terms, he made recommendations to parents in handling childhood problems through manipulation rewards and punishments. Perhaps his most well-known paper was the demonstration that even emotions could be learned, flying in the face of the psychoanalytic dogma of the day (Watson, 1924).

Less flamboyant and never recognized for his accomplishments in his own day, Leightner Witmer founded the first American psychological clinic at the University of Pennsylvania in 1896. Witmer developed assessment techniques, counseled with parents, and developed a special class for teachers in the evaluation and teaching of children. Witmer was ahead of his time in diagnosing learning disabilities, mental retardation, and exceptionally bright children. He labeled his approach to understanding and treating learning difficulties in the classroom as "orthogenics" and founded a journal to disseminate his methods (Gardner, 1968; Baker, 1988).

## *CONTEMPORARY APPROACHES*

From these beginnings, an attitude of treatment rather than discipline and understanding rather than condemnation emerged. Children previously regarded merely as unpleasant were now seen as troubled and in need of intervention by mental health professionals. Kazdin (1988) points out that there are literally hundreds of types of psychotherapy available for children, yet there is a dearth of empirical outcome studies that would make it possible to compare the effectiveness of therapeutic techniques. Three major groupings of these therapies may be labeled "psychodynamic," "cognitive-behavioral," and "family systems" therapies. In practice, many clinicians are eclectic, drawing upon many approaches to get the job accomplished rather than remaining within the constraints of any one theoretical system. Differences between experienced and novice therapists within any one theoretical system of psychotherapy may be greater than differences between experienced therapists of different theoretical persuasions.

Pyschodynamic approaches to children, as with any other approach, are limited by the cognitive development of the child and must rely heavily upon play, storytelling, and other ways to engage children in the therapeutic process. Material produced by the child is not accepted at face value but rather in terms of deeper meanings of which the child may be unaware. The mere treatment of symptoms or behaviors is regarded as superficial. Therapists accepting a psychodynamic model believe that unresolved conflicts producing symptoms, if left untreated, will continue to affect behavior. If symptoms alone are treated, symptom substitution may result. The relationship evolving in therapy between the child and the therapist is viewed as critical to outcome. Through this "transference" relationship the child acts out important conflicts with parents or other significant persons.

Behavioral approaches, based upon empirical studies of learning, emphasize the current behavior of the child rather than underlying conflicts originating in early childhood. The immediate stimulus conditions precipitating the behavior as well as the immediate consequences of the behavior are of primary significance. Most behavior is assumed to be learned on the basis of contingent reinforcement and maintained by its consequences. Behavioral interventions are designed to eliminate (extinguish) the behavior by withdrawal of the reinforcement or to teach new, more adaptive behaviors that are incompatible with the inappropriate behaviors. Target behaviors are viewed as functional to the child, i.e., in service of some basic need or motivation. Behavior analysis is the method of determining both the stimulus conditions and reinforcements operating within the natural environment that serve to maintain the behavior. This is analogous to the evaluation phase of more traditional therapeutic approaches. Strict behavioral approaches may be limited to situations in which control of situations and outcomes is possible over long periods of time. Generalization to other settings where such control is not possible may be problematic. Behavior modification was a popular and effective approach within mental hospitals and institutions for mentally retarded persons for many years when deinstitutionalization was not a widely available option.

In recent years, behavioral approaches have been greatly influenced by cognitive psychology. Cognitive-behavioral approaches have become widely accepted by psychologists unwilling to ignore feelings and cognitions as part of the therapeutic process. Cognitive-behavioral approaches attempt to change feelings and behavior when necessary by teaching the individual to challenge his or her own cognitions if they are irrational or illogical. Cognitive theorists believe that many people learn to accept distorted views of themselves in early childhood, and such damaging cognitions operate as a kind of internal tape recording, influencing behavior and feelings. Cognitive therapists teach clients to reexamine these cognitions and to empirically test them if necessary. For example, a student who fails an examination may conclude, "I failed because I am stupid." This cognition, learned early in life, implies, "I will always be stupid" and "I will always fail." A more reasonable explanation may be "I failed because I didn't study hard enough, but I can do better next time." Cognitive-behavior therapy primarily deals with the here and now and targets behavioral outcomes that can be objectively measured.

Family systems approaches conceptualize the child's problems only in the context of the family and as intergenerational. Parents are not blamed for the problem but neither is the child. Rather, dysfunctional behavior is seen as only the visible manifestation of a broader family dysfunctioning. The roles each family member plays in the problem and their interactions are given highest priority. Family therapists are well aware of the fact that a child's problem, targeted by the family, may merely be a convenient focus for a broader and unverbalized family problem.

It is common in child psychotherapy to find that alleviation of the troublesome behavior in the child is closely followed by the exacerbation of another problem in a sibling or one of the parents. In one case, a child was having learning and behavioral problems. These problems showed dramatic improvement when the child was engaged in individual psychotherapy. Shortly after this, the parents announced they were contemplating a divorce. By focusing upon the child, the family was masking the more serious marital conflicts that were being expressed at home and were affecting the child. How relevant are these approaches for children in the child welfare system? In many cases, families are not available to be involved in therapy. Therapists at residential treatment facilities attempt to apply whatever approaches for which they have been trained. There are no therapies specific to children placed into custody. Perhaps there should be. Chapter 8 presents a cognitive therapy approach to such children based upon internal cognitions that are expressed by the children or presumed from their histories.

## RESIDENTIAL TREATMENT

Barker (1974) describes the residential treatment of children with conduct disorder diagnoses in a psychiatric unit at the Maudsley Hospital in London. He defines conduct disorder as a cluster of repetitive behavior patterns that are antisocial and disapproved. "A characteristic common to all these children on admission is their experience of conflict, misunderstanding and failure in their relationship with adults . . . " (p. 49). Their behavior involved "acting out" against people or property, was persistent, and failed to respond to normal sanctions. Baker lists a variety of predisposing causes of conduct disorder, including cerebral dysfunction, but places considerable emphasis upon a deficiency of stable, affectionate care as a common factor. Admission to the Maudsley inpatient psychiatric unit is based upon the following conditions: the child's behavior is unacceptable in a nonpsychiatric setting; the child is a danger to himself or to others; behavior is bizarre or irrational; behavior is deteriorating or failing to respond to ordinary measures available in the community; and treatment can be done only as an inpatient. Contraindications for admission are: the absence of a home for visits and community contacts; the absence of an adult in the community to be concerned about his or her well-being; admission would damage the child's relationships in the community; the child cannot accept the admission except as punishment; and the behavior is confined to stealing in a child deprived of affection. Barker sees the benefits of inpatient treatment as deriving from the temporary removal of the child from an unsuitable environment; the provision of structure, supervision, and control within a therapeutic environment; and the provision of active treatment and opportunity for continued development.

The program at Maudsley combines structure with flexibility in discipline that allows for relationship building and a therapeutic milieu, a balance between tolerance and self-expression with organization and limit setting. Children are encouraged to express fears and resentment and to participate in decision making. Group meetings for counseling and social interactions are heavily relied upon. The program is run according to a medical model with ultimate responsibility for the treatment belonging to the psychiatrist. However, treatment is viewed as a team process including the teacher, occupational therapist, psychologist, psychiatric social worker, and nurse. Links with the community, liaisons with other social agencies, and trial visits home are an integral part of the program and are the responsibility of the social worker. Medication is also relied upon, but traditional forms of psychotherapy may be thwarted by acting-out children. Brief (three-minute) "time-out" periods for misbehavior are also found to be useful. Nurses, who appear to be the primary caregivers, are instructed to be tolerant of the wrongdoer but to always demonstrate a better way. School is designed to be a happy place where learning is offered but not forced down the child's throat. Date for discharge is set at the time of admission. Difficulty encountered with the child on the ward does not necessarily predict outcome.

Unsuccessful outcomes are seen as largely related to the type of home and community situations to which the children return. However, definitive follow-up studies are lacking. Furthermore, although it is understandable that children without viable homes or interested families might be denied access to the program, that type of exclusion would eliminate many of the children needing placement.

## EFFECTIVENESS OF TREATMENT MODELS

Kutash (1995) presents a review of the effectiveness of children's mental health services, reviewing eight service components for children, including residential treatment, outpatient psychotherapy, day treatment, family preservation (homebound), therapeutic foster care, crisis intervention, case management, and family support services. The overall conclusions are limited because of an insufficient database deriving from controlled clinical studies, both under laboratory and clinic conditions in the community. Kutash notes the lack of confidence that many clinicians have for controlled outcome studies and the need for greater rapprochement between researchers and clinicians. The need for investigations, not only of individual service components but also of broad systems of care integrating several components, is indicated. I refer next to results of only two service components from Kutash's extensive review—residential services and outpatient psychotherapy.

The review of residential services lumps together studies of psychiatric hospitals and residential treatment centers. Mixed evidence exists of the effectiveness of residential treatment to no treatment. Kutash concludes "that there is no conclusive evidence to support the effectiveness of residential treatment over other treatment settings" (1995, p. 445). Factors that appear to be predictive of positive outcomes of residential services include adequate intelligence, nonpsychotic and nonorganic diagnoses, the absence of bizarre and antisocial behaviors, healthy family functioning, adequate length of stay, specialized treatment regimen, availability of after-care services, and less severe child and family dysfunction. One is tempted to ask, if these factors are valid in predicting success, why was the child receiving residential care in the first place? Factors predictive of poor prognosis were poor initial response to treatment, a diagnosis of ADHD, older age at admission, childhood depression, presence of neurological or psychotic symptoms, limited after-care treatment, a history of physical abuse, and higher intellectual functioning. The most positive conclusion drawn by Kutash is that residential services have resulted in improved functioning for some children.

Earlier studies of the effectiveness of outpatient psychotherapy yielded negative findings. However, more recent, laboratory-based, controlled studies suggest an overall positive effect of psychotherapy with children. Meta-analyses of such studies (i.e., analyses lumping together results of several similar studies) report positive outcomes for the use of psychotherapy with children as compared with children not receiving treatment for comparable conditions. Controlled research studies tend to be performed more frequently with therapists using structured, cognitive, and cognitive-behavioral approaches. Community-based studies, which are less well controlled and tend to use more eclectic methods, yield less positive results. The need for the expansion of clinic-based research is emphasized.

# Chapter 8

# A Cognitive Therapy Approach

"Are you still enamored of cognitive approaches to therapy?"

"Yes. The strict behavioral approach just seems to be not sufficient for these kids. We can control contingencies to some degree here, but not rigidly. Monetary rewards have limited effectiveness because the children get money from home. The fifty cents a day for good behavior is just not very powerful, especially if accounting is late in getting us the funds for payoffs. Even if we can gain some behavioral control of the kids while they are here, it doesn't generalize. We can work with families but not schools and neighborhoods. If the kids don't internalize some rules to carry with them when they leave, I think the experience here is limited."

"Won't they learn the rules by experience? If a boy gets caught stealing and spends time in juvenile detention, isn't that a more powerful learning opportunity than whatever verbalizations you teach them?"

"We've had kids sent to the juvenile detention center after serious episodes, and they were well behaved when they returned. They appreciated their relative freedom in our program after 'lock-up.' But it didn't last. Punishment or the fear of punishment is effective in suppressing behavior, but remove the threat and the behavior returns. I'd be more optimistic about changing cognitions."

"If you can really do that."

\* \* \*

We try to arrive at a dynamic formulation about the children in the RTF and why they behave as they do. Luke's concerns seem to drive him to be defiant and the toughest kid around. He is worried about his height. Basically, however, he is concerned about abandonment. He has been able to verbalize concern about what would happen to him should his foster mother die. He knows he is a foster child and cannot see his natural mother. Separations, therefore, are difficult. At first we thought it was only a transition. That was the reason we arrived at for his resistance about going home on weekends. Now we understand that his resistance is a mechanism of control. If he refuses to go home, it precludes his mother refusing to take him home. Luke recognizes his precarious position in life. Fortunately, his mom has been able to reassure him that she is in good health and were she not, one of his foster brothers would assume responsibility for him. Yet, by opposing adult authority, even for inconsequential requests, Luke maintains his sense of control.

*    *    *

Psychiatric diagnoses often reflect the orientation and biases of the facility at which they are made. While the children of the RTF represent the broad gamut of classifications used currently in psychiatry, they fall roughly into two broad categories. The children with Attention Deficit Hyperactivity Disorder are in most ways the more difficult ones. As adolescents, they also demonstrate the antisocial and personality disorders that ADHD may spawn, but their most obvious characteristic is their impulsivity. They are like a coiled spring with potential energy always ready to be unleashed. They must touch everything. They cannot sit still. Therapy is a challenge to child and therapist. Children with oppositional, defiant, and conduct disorders are always ready to instigate trouble. Children with ADHD eagerly follow their lead. Of course, some children show both types of disorder. Stealing, setting fires, destroying property, and aggressive acts are not regarded by these children as antisocial but rather as "cool."

Those are the obvious—the observable behaviors. These behaviors anger staff from other buildings and sometimes result in ostracism by the other clients. Scrape the surface and you see much more.

When an adult is hurt, he or she usually has the resources to cope, to defend against the incident so that it does not become a blow to his or her ego. He or she can put the incident in perspective by blaming others and by seeing the situation as finite and time limited. Not so a child—hurts can be enduring in childhood because children do not have the cognitive resources to understand. Still, in the process of learning about the world, they incorporate the hurt as part of their life view. Worse yet, they may blame themselves for the trauma. They were hurt because they deserved it. Once burned, they will always be vulnerable and so they build up the best defenses they can muster. They become tough, distrusting, belligerent, and eternally vigilant against further assaults. They hoard weapons, ever ready to unleash their arsenals against new perpetrators, and all adults are potential enemies.

Let there be no misunderstanding. These children are damaged. Sometimes the damage is physical. Children of mothers using crack or alcohol during pregnancy, providing little prenatal care, and further neglecting or abusing their infants come out impaired. It may not be the obvious brain damage or physical impairments of the most severely handicapped child but rather more subtle manifestations. Hyperactivity, learning disabilities, and difficulties in processing information are often characteristic of these children. Emotional damage is less easy to document.

Each of the kids at the RTF needs to be the toughest kid on the block. It is often no more than posturing and bravado, but they will fight when challenged with a ferocity that only children can generate. The reaction often seems to far exceed the provocation, for it is not the target they are really angry at but rather a world they see as hostile and threatening. Deep down, even they know this to be true. Divided against one another, they are problematic but manageable. Yet, it is when they band together and become a gang that our best staff become helpless and immobilized. But beneath this anger, beneath the armor that hides the hurt, is a soft underbelly of a child crying out to be loved.

Children who are out of control, children who often cannot control their own bodily movements, need to control others. Children who find they have become powerful, even over those they most fear, those in authority, are frightened by their power. Some children constantly test their environment, as with Rich who introduced our first therapy session with "You know I smoke." He produced a cigarette lighter from his pocket to prove his point. His challenge went unanswered. "Do you like it?" I asked. "No. Luke gets me to do it." There are children who want their world to become consistent, predictable, fair, and limit setting—children who themselves become alarmed when their friends become less controlled than they, saying, "Put them in restraints."

More than any other population we have encountered, welfare children demonstrate an inordinate need for attention. No matter how successful they become at gaining it, they are a bottomless pit eager for more. Unmet needs for nurturance early in life leave a child with a sense of emptiness that cannot be satiated. This manifests itself as a preoccupation with material possessions. Buy the child a present today, and he or she will look in your hands tomorrow. When there is no hope of being given something material, he or she will find ways of negotiating privileges. Those means exhausted, the child will dare any transgression to gain peer approval, status, recognition, and adult attention—even negative attention. The child seems repeatedly to be saying, "Notice me. Here I am. Acknowledge my being. Compensate me for what I have missed, for I too have needs. I, who have been hurt, must be given my due. Give it to me now, or I will take it." From the first encounter with such children, you will be tested. Their trust is a precious commodity to them and they relinquish it grudgingly. They make the rules, not you. And in the hierarchy of priorities, peer approval stands high and conformity to societal expectations ranks near the bottom of the list.

However, a high priority is also a desire to appear normal when they are in the public eye. The worst thing that can happen to them is to be singled out in public as someone who is abnormal or deviant, as happened to Luke, who went with the group on a trip to the Philadelphia zoo. While the rest of the kids and staff were enjoying the new lion cubs, Luke decided he wanted to see the bears and went off by himself to do so. Staff members, concerned that he would become lost, tried to restrain him physically. Luke became hysterical—biting, scratching, and flailing around in his humiliation. They had crossed the line, and he lost all control.

## TREATMENT ISSUES

Residential treatment of these children raises many practical questions with few easy answers. Do these children get better with treatment? What are the criteria of improvement? If their behavior improves in a treatment setting, will the new behavior generalize to their family and community settings? How do we prepare them to return to many of the same conditions in which their disturbance originated.

When residential treatment works, it is because we are in the position of doing certain things that don't happen at home. Surrogate parents and authority figures are provided. They are in a position to model new behaviors for the children. If they act in ways similar to the family or other adults who have abused them in the past, the effort is lost and residential treatment only confirms what the children already know: "This is a hostile world, and I can trust no one."

The children can obtain realistic feedback about how they and their behavior is received by a new set of adults who are responsible for them. This experience expands their knowledge about life in general and how they fit into the order of things. They quickly learn who likes them and who doesn't, whom they can manipulate, and who runs things. Again, if this new environment merely replicates their past experience, treatment is bound to fail.

Treatment can provide a safe, consistent, predictable, nurturing, and nonjudgmental environment. This is perhaps the most difficult condition to arrange. It is no secret that sometimes children are not well-received by staff. Sometimes they are treated poorly, even abused. Sometimes the well-meaning treatment of professionals is misguided as either excessively punitive or excessively permissive. How do we balance the need of children for discipline and their need for acceptance and love? How do we protect them from one another as each struggles to maintain his or her image of toughness and invincibility.

Treatment needs to provide limit setting and predictable, consistent outcomes for behavior—outcomes that approximate what exists in the real world. Treatment should convey acceptance of the child, although not always acceptance of his or her behavior. Children naturally band into small groups that they accept as family. Somehow, children in treatment need to include the staff, and especially their therapists, into something similar to a family to which they feel some ties. For that to happen, staff need to communicate a degree of liking and acceptance. This is the most difficult of tasks since staff also represent authority, limits, restraint, and discipline.

Treatment must reinforce the notion that self-scrutiny and self-monitoring are expected. Abused and neglected children are ever ready to blame others for their condition. Therapy assumes that, to some extent, behaviors are a matter of personal choice so that, with insight, children may regulate and improve their behaviors. Children must be able to say, "Yes, there is something wrong with my behavior. Yet I am in control and willing to try to change for the better." This does not happen overnight. For some, it never happens. Yet, the ultimate discharge of the child back to his or her family or to a less restrictive setting should be based on this process.

Treatment can teach anger recognition and methods of non-aggressive expression of anger. Treatment can provide opportunities for the family and child to relate differently toward each other. This means perceiving each other differently, hopefully in a more positive light. The issues addressed here concern the approach to therapy that is evolving, as well as the development of criteria for evaluating progress and for decision making regarding exit from the program. Although the frequency and severity of aggressive and destructive behaviors could serve as one criterion, the therapeutic nature of the program demanded the use of more cognitive indexes as well. Cognitive and cognitive-behavior therapy appeared to offer both a rationale and a strategic approach to therapy, but specific procedures fitted to the histories and behaviors of these children needed to be designed.

## COGNITIVE THERAPY

Various forms of cognitive therapy have been elaborated by Beck and colleagues (1979), Ellis (1974), Lazarus (1976), and Meichenbaum (1977). In general, emphasis is placed on the potency of cognitions, in the form of ideas, attitudes, beliefs, or other pervasive thoughts that become automatic over a lifetime and occur specifically in certain critical situations. Such cognitions are assumed to be closely associated with both emotions and behaviors so that, once aroused, they may elicit emotional and behavioral reactions. Such automatic thoughts may become the basis of a life motif that influences every sphere of one's life and are accepted by the individual without challenge. When such thoughts represent illogical or distorted perceptions of reality, they may form the basis of emotional disorder. Beck has developed cognitive approaches to therapy that assist the individual in empirically validating these cognitions. Initially applied to depression, this technique has been expanded by Beck to deal with anxiety as well as personality disorders. Research tends to support the efficacy of cognitive approaches to levels equivalent to the use of psychotropic medication.

Group counseling within a cognitive therapy framework has been used with mentally and emotionally disturbed offenders with a special management unit of a state prison (Scott, 1993). The importance of "talking out" rather than "acting out" is stressed. "Offenders need not only to change their behavior (keep the rules, etc.), but more important, their attitude/mind. If this distinction is not operative, *offenders might be better prisoners, but not better people. . . .* Behavior in prison can be modified by psychotropic medication, by lock-up, by restrictions, but not necessarily by the offender's attitude. Some offenders are good at 'Programming,' looking good for the parole board, but there might be no attitudinal change. Behavior is overt. Attitude tends to be covert, and often difficult to judge" (Scott, 1993, p. 133).

Gries (1986) describes the use of multiple goals in the treatment of foster children with emotional disorders—children with histories of physical and emotional abuse similar to those in RTFs. Gries points out that these children often blame themselves for their displacement from home. Such a cognition may result in low self-esteem, disillusionment, and confusion. Conflict may be generated by their unmet needs for nurturance from their natural parents and patterns of avoidance of those persons by whom they have been abused. The child often harbors fantasies about a reconciliation with the natural parent. "He or she typically becomes entrapped in the conflicted webs of approach tendencies (regaining feelings of acceptance by the parent), avoidance tendencies (averting further painful experiences with the parent), and attack tendencies (seeking revenge for past painful experiences)" (Gries, 1986, p. 381).

Adjustment problems in the foster home may stem from the tenuous position the children occupy when parents implicitly or explicitly communicate, "Consider this your home, unless you misbehave." Gries defines several treatment goals with these children. Children need to gain a clear understanding of the reasons for their placement. They need help in relating in a trusting manner and in communicating feelings and desires. They need to regain some measure of control of their own lives in making decisions and learning that they have power to influence outcomes of their behavior. They need to verbalize positive feelings about themselves. Finally, they need to be desensitized to the avoidant and even phobic reactions they have developed toward their parents.

### Facilitating Cognitive Change

Abandoned and abused children manifesting conduct and other related behavioral disorders also develop certain cognitions about themselves and their environments, usually for good reasons. These cognitions, shared by many of the children, appear to have a close relationship to their repeated defiance of rules and authority figures. These cognitions often include the convictions that they are basically bad or inadequate; they are unloved and unwanted; people are not to be trusted; the world is a hostile and dangerous place; their only defense is to strike out first; they are usually helpless and have no control over their lives except through defiance; their world is unstable and unreliable; and they have no real future. Being able to change such devastating thoughts may require more than therapeutic efforts; it may require radical changes in the children's environments as well. For this reason, the involvement of families in the therapeutic process is essential. Cognitive therapy requires identification of the child's inappropriate cognitions and the rehearsal of more realistic and adaptive thoughts.

By paying attention to the child's verbalizations, a therapist or program manager can gain insights into the child's acceptance of the treatment program and progress he or she might be making. One child who was resisting any participation in family meetings finally blurted out, "I can change if I want to . . . ," leaving unsaid but strongly implying that he, in fact, did not want to change. Although the statement was thrown out angrily, in a posture of defiance, we felt it was a positive sign that he recognized change was being asked of him and that he had the capability for such change. Later in treatment, the same child asked whether a change in his behavior would make him a different person or would he still be the same person. We interpreted that question as an indication of the anxiety he felt about relinquishing his defiance posture but also considered it as a positive sign that he was even contemplating change. This child did begin to show significant change in controlling severe, explosive reactions of anger. His verbalizations mirrored this improvement as he began to refer to his old self and his new self. "I used to do those things, but I don't do them anymore."

This approach has led us to identify therapeutic change as a twelve-step process in which the child accepts as his or her own the following sequence of cognitions:

1. My behavior is socially unacceptable, inappropriate, wrong, self-defeating, and out of control.
2. I am responsible for my own behavior.
3. My life might be better if I change in ways suggested by the staff.
4. I want to change.
5. I am capable of change.
6. The specific behaviors I want to change are . . .
7. My staff (therapist) is here to help me change.
8. This is what I must do . . .
9. I can keep track of my progress by . . .
10. I am making progress in these behaviors . . .
11. My behavior is now more acceptable to others.
12. I am beginning to like myself better.

When children are able to genuinely accept these thoughts about themselves, they have, indeed, changed for the better. They have restructured their perceptions of themselves despite their histories, genes, and diagnoses. It is not a question of what particular solutions society imposes upon them but rather the children's internal, cognitive view of themselves in their world that counts.

The treatment of children who have been sexually or physically abused also follows these guidelines but has its own set of cognitions to be learned. Victims need to tell themselves:

1. I am still a good person.
2. I am the same person I was before.

3. It was not my fault.
4. It must not happen again.
5. I can prevent it from happening again.
6. I am safe now.
7. It need not affect my future.
8. I know where to get help if I need it.
9. I am going on with my life.

Children who have been perpetrators need to tell themselves:

1. Some things I have done are unacceptable.
2. I do not wish to hurt anyone (as I have been hurt).
3. I must change my behavior.
4. I am capable of controlling my behavior.
5. I know where to get help.
6. I am still a good person.
7. I can still go on with my life.

### Success Factors

Subjectively, and without empirical validation so far, we attribute treatment gains to the following factors:

- Children begin to recognize that they are not the worst kids on the block. Their peers in the program have similar or worse problems. At home or in the local school, the child is usually identified as a severe behavior problem. He or she accepts this role and believes it to be pervasive, enduring, and due to his or her own basic inferiority. It sometimes comes as a revelation that other children may be demonstrating behavior worse than his or her own.
- The RTF program provides a sense of stability and consistency. Although planned as a short-term treatment program (up to eighteen months), some children may stay longer. The consistency of staff and procedures contrasts sharply with the instability of repeated foster placements or psychiatric hospitalizations. Again, involving families affords credibility to the program. This is a real part of life, not just another way station. Cognitive therapy adds greatly to program effectiveness.

- The children develop a sense of loyalty to each other. They learn not to steal from each other and to respect boundaries. They develop into a gang that is more powerful and more destructive than its individual members. This creates an administrative problem, but it is therapeutic for the children. They treat each other as a family and become protective. For some, it may be the only sense of family they have ever had. If we are lucky, as staff, we may be accepted as somewhat distant relatives in this family—tolerated, if not respected. Some of us may eventually be trusted.
- The program provides a sense of safety. Many of the children live in neighborhoods that are little short of battlegrounds. The children know they will not be harmed at the center. They also learn that staff intend to help them, even if they continue to rebel against the rules.
- The program provides an exit. Discharge is planned from the time of arrival. Goals for each child are presented repeatedly by staff as the means to an end. Discharge is not just another placement. Rather, it is a step forward in their lives—a move toward greater independence, maturity, employment, and acceptance.

# Chapter 9

# Teaching Values

"So, behavior modification isn't enough for you. You want kids to internalize values—to discriminate right from wrong and buy into the American dream by becoming good citizens. Are you practicing religion or psychology?"

"You know better than that. If behavior modification could provide kids the motivation to be socialized, I'd say use whatever works. But we don't have that much control. Cognitive psychology adds to the power of the technology. We, as psychologists, need not be ashamed to embrace what religion and morality endorse."

"The values you are interested in teaching may merely be abstractions of specific behaviors. Do you remember the old Hartshorn and May character trait studies? The issue was the generality of so-called traits such as honesty. Do kids who steal from the Red Cross collection envelope also illicitly change their wrong answers on a test? If I recall, there was little correlation among specific dishonest acts. It was an attack upon Allport's (1961) trait theory. You may be trying to teach something that doesn't exist."

"Now who's getting preachy? Don't quote fifty-year-old studies to me. They weren't the final word. The values I am addressing are broader than honesty, although honesty is important. There is more than behavior involved here. Children need to be motivated to consider the rights of others. They need to incorporate all the thou shalts and shalt nots so that even if they transgress (and that depends upon many factors) they will know they have done something wrong and will feel remorse. They need to be concerned about helping others. They must want to control their anger and learn to resolve conflicts peacefully. Actually, the issue of whether these are general or specific characteristics of the child is not relevant here. The concern is whether for each of these types of behaviors the child will develop some internal processing mechanism needed to regulate his or her behavior and be inclined to do so."

## THE RELEVANCE OF VALUES

Contemporary treatment programs, strongly influenced by behavioral psychology, have focused primarily upon skill training of children and families (Bloomquist, 1996). Children are instructed in strategies for anger management, parents in coping mechanisms for behavior control and in mechanisms of stress reduction. Contingency management such as levels systems is highly relied upon within the RTF in order to provide children with clear expectations for the consequences of their behavior. The need for structure, consistency for children, and the provision of staff with powerful technologies for control are emphasized.

The treatment literature is less oriented toward the teaching of values, standards, and internalized control mechanisms, although it may be implicitly assumed that external limits will result in the incorporation of internal mechanisms, much as a young child learns to incorporate societal standards during early developmental stages. One exception to this trend is the approach of Brendtro, Brokenleg, and Van Bockern (1990).

Yet, the teaching of values is not foreign to psychologists and educators. The emphasis on "moral training" in early residential programs (Reeder, 1909) has been described in Chapter 1. The learning of values such as altruism and empathy has been studied by developmental psychologists (Kohlberg, 1969; Piaget, 1955). Moral valuation (Stilwell et al., 1996) is the process of formulating rules that are internalized and used as standards to guide behavior. Research findings (Stilwell et al., 1996) suggest a developmental process beginning with the unquestioning acceptance of an external authority for rules through the internalization of rules that may be self-formulated and altered. Increasing attention is being paid to the teaching of morals to children (Coles, 1997).

Moral valuation is the process of justifying the moral rules (i.e., principles, beliefs) that are associated with defining one's self as a good person who strives to do the right thing. In the valuation process, one justifies following or not following learned moral rules, sometimes modifying a rule in the process. Justifications involve more than moral reasoning (i.e., applying one's best cognitive abilities to determining what makes a particular value right or wrong). The justification process also involves psychological defenses (e.g., denial, projection, rationalization), temperamental characteristics (e.g., impulsivity, inhibition), and psychophysiological responses (e.g., stress, fatigue). Stages of moral valuation are elaborated. The instrument is a fifteen-question SCI (Stilwell Conscience Inventory) that assesses five domains of conscience functioning in children and adolescents: conceptualization, moral-emotional responsiveness, moral valuation, internalization of moral attachment, and moral volition. Three questions are related to moral valuation:

- What are the main principles (rules, dos, and don'ts) in your conscience?
- Which person(s) has(ve) helped the most in putting the rules in your conscience?
- Sometimes there are good reasons for obeying rules; sometimes there are good reasons for not obeying rules. Let's look at your rules and see what you think about them. What are your best reasons for obeying rules? What are your best reasons for not obeying rules? (Stilwell et al.,1996)

Emotionally disturbed children may be in a less mature moral development system or may be locked into a deviant but no less sophisticated rule system. Altruism and empathy in children diagnosed with conduct or other behavioral disorders may be less prepotent than rules dictated by a gang subculture. The objective of "moral training" was more than merely teaching a discrimination of right from wrong. More important was instilling the motivation to behave according to moral and ethical standards. Addressing processing of moral valuation in a behaviorally disturbed population would seem to require changes in basic generalizations about the world.

Altruism refers to behavior intended to help others at some cost or risk to oneself and with no obvious benefits to oneself. Some psychologists have argued that altruism really does not exist, i.e., that such behavior is in the service of self-interest, although the benefits may be subtle or anticipated for the future. The critical factor would be what the person who performs the altruistic deed tells him- or herself. Nevertheless, acts of heros and seemingly unselfish behaviors do occur, extending beyond the family circle. Sabini (1992) observes that altruism serves to perpetuate the species. Others have explained selfless acts on the basis of psychological rather than material gain. Helping people provides pleasure, and failure to help may produce pain (Bateson, 1987). Research with infants demonstrates that a child will cry at the sound of another infant crying (Sagi and Hoffman, 1976). Thus, relieving another's distress may serve to relieve our own distress as well. Subjects will learn a sequence of button pressing faster if they perceive that it will terminate another person's pain than if it has no effect upon their pain (Geer and Jermecky, 1973).

The concept of empathy is obviously related to that of altruism, but there is disagreement as to how it should be defined. Some would define empathy as an understanding and compassion for another's distress. Others reserve the term empathy for those situations in which a person not only understands and cares about another's distress but also shares it. Still others would term the previous situations as *sympathy*, reserving the term *empathy* for situations in which the person is also motivated to relieve the distress of the other person. Conflicting evidence exists as to whether empathy is based upon a drive to elevate one's own mood (Cialdini et al., 1987; Batson et al., 1989).

How relevant are these motives for emotionally disturbed adolescents? Anecdotal evidence suggests that the RTF residents in our program demonstrate both altruism and empathy. One child, whose foster mother took him home almost every weekend, asked his mother to also provide weekends home for his friend who never went home. This request was repeated even though the first child complained that the second child touched his toys and generally got in his way. Children in the unit act in very protective ways toward those they feel are being abused or exploited. Terry had consistently bullied Carrie until she saw Carrie being strong-armed by her mother. After that, Terry became protective of her. Are the children merely doing what is expected of them, or do they truly empathize with victims? Can altruism and empathy be taught?

## DEVELOPMENTAL STAGES

Stages of moral development have been outlined by Kohlberg (1969) using a measure of moral judgment as a criterion. Kohlberg makes it clear that moral judgment is not identical with moral action but may be a necessary but not sufficient condition for moral action. The evaluation of the level of moral judgment of a child is conducted by using a series of moral-ethical dilemmas. One example is that of a man who robs a drugstore of a cancer medication to save his wife's life when no other possibility of obtaining the drug was available. The child is asked is describe and defend the best course of action for each hypothetical situation. Kohlberg identifies six stages of moral judgment, with the first two stages representing judgments based upon consequences to the individual rather than the incorporation of underlying values. The highest stages represent an orientation toward society's rules, universal principles of justice, and respect for the rights and dignity of others.

A study by Gregg, Gibbs, and Basinger (1994) utilized a modified Kohlberg-like scale, the Sociomoral Reflection Measure, to compare a group of male and female delinquent adolescents comparable in age, socioeconomic status, and verbal IQ. Seven moral value areas were assessed: contract, truth, affiliation, life, property, law, and legal justice. Delinquent and nondelinquent males and females were compared. The development of moral judgment of both male and female delinquent (or conduct disorder) groups was significantly lower than that of the nondelinquent controls. Less than 20 percent of the delinquent groups scored higher than Stage 2. In both delinquent and nondelinquent groups, the moral judgment of males was less advanced than that of females. Delinquents of both genders were particularly low scoring in valuing the importance of obeying the law. Certain values were generally high, even in the delinquent groups. These included keeping a promise, helping others, and saving a life, suggesting that these values may be generally pervasive. Although the delinquent and nondelinquent groups were not perfectly matched (the delinquents were primarily disadvantaged and black, the nondelinquents, primarily middle-class and white), the differences in moral judgments in these two groups suggest that moral judgment is related to moral behavior.

## *TWO VALUES FOR STUDY*

The development of values such as altruism and empathy has been researched so that some of the factors determining behaviors reflecting such values are known. For a child to empathize with others and to behave in an altruistic fashion, certain developmental milestones must be attained. The child must be able to overcome an egocentric focus and be able to see the world as others see it. Piaget and Inhelder (1956) assumed that perceptual and cognitive structures required for this ability were equivalent (i.e., develop at the same time) and that such structures are not in place until the age of seven. Today, developmental psychologists realize that perceptual and cognitive egocentrism are overcome at separate times and probably at ages younger than seven. The motive to help others seems to be a complex phenomenon that depends upon many factors, both developmentally as well as situationally. Children may behave in a generous fashion, for example, more out of a desire to meet the expectations of others than as an expression of a genuine altruistic motive. As mentioned earlier, another factor may be the mood of the individual when the opportunity to behave altruistically arises. Both good and bad moods may serve to elicit altruism, presumably to maintain a good feeling in the first case and to remove a bad feeling in the latter.

The development of altruism in children depends primarily upon the availability of role models who display this value. Research suggests that important factors are the degree to which parents are affectionate with their children (Hoffman, 1975), the degree to which they explain the connection between behavior of the child and the feelings of others (Hoffman, 1975; Zahn-Waxler, Radke-Yarrow, and King, 1979), and the degree to which parents themselves value altruism (Hoffman, 1975). Presumably, the mechanisms by which parents teach altruism include explicit reinforcement of altruistic behavior and implicit modeling of altruistic behavior. When families are dysfunctional, when they are involved in antisocial behaviors themselves, or when they are simply not available, it is not surprising that their offspring fail to learn these lessons.

## *MORAL TRAINING*

Chapter 1 discussed that schools accepted responsibility for moral training during the nineteenth century. The teaching of good citizenship was identified by educators as a priority for all children, and that influence is still apparent in public education today. The issue has some political implications because of sensitivities over cultural differences so that sometimes the teaching of morals is disguised in curricula as "ethics and community living."

Curwin (1993) describes the provision of "helping opportunities" to at-risk children in order to help them overcome feelings of worthlessness. Such opportunities must be genuine rather than artificial, optional to the student, and make reasonable demands upon the child. Examples used were helping younger children, giving performances for hospitalized children, raising money for charity, and assisting nursing home residents. Curwin describes the strategy as a powerful intervention for replacing anger with caring.

Coles (1997) addresses the issue of the moral conduct of children and how it develops in response to the ways in which the child is treated at home:

> Moral intelligence is not acquired only by memorization of rules and regulations, by dint of abstract classroom discussion or kitchen compliance. We grow morally as a consequence of learning how to be with others, how to behave in this world, a learning prompted by taking to heart what we have seen and heard. The child is a witness; the child is an ever-attentive witness of grown-up morality—or lack thereof; the child looks and looks for cues as to how one ought to behave, as we parents and teachers go about our lives, making choices, addressing people, showing in action our rock-bottom assumptions, desires, and values, and thereby telling those young observers much more than they may realize. (p. 5)

Coles challenges parents and teachers to provide children with moral as well as cognitive direction—to find creative ways to teach children to live by the Golden Rule, to learn to get along with others, and to be able to discriminate the characteristics of the "good person" from the "not-so-good" person.

Even psychologists are not immune from disregarding, or at least failing to consider, the moral underpinnings of their profession. In a recent article, Prilleltensky (1997) urges psychologists to appraise the moral implications of their work. "Psychologists are not alone in their pursuit of a moral compass. We share with the larger community a moral illiteracy fueled by cultural and political trends that undermine our moral competence" (p. 517). Prilleltensky suggests a set of values useful to psychologists, defining moral values as benefits that human beings provide to other individuals and communities. These values include caring and compassion, self-determination, human diversity, collaboration and democratic participation, and distributive justice.

Hogan (1993) addresses the question of whether "moral deviants" can be educated. In the absence of strong empirical evidence, drawn primarily from the field of criminal corrections, he determines that there is little basis on which to conclude that rehabilitation efforts are successful. On the basis of theoretical considerations, he speculates about what would be necessary to bring about such positive change. His reasoning is based upon the following assumptions:

1. It is not the knowledge of right and wrong that is deficient in deviant persons.
2. Knowledge of social standards does not indicate compliance. Criminals can often give all the right answers to questions dealing with moral valuation.
3. Rather, to bring about significant change in moral behavior it would be necessary to make changes in character structure.
4. During early years, moral development requires compliance with adult authority. During teenage years, moral development entails concern over social approval, particularly peer approval.
5. Moral development at the highest level (compliance with an abstract principle) is a function of intelligence, not character.
6. Persons who start out as socially deviant and later become good citizens attach themselves to a group that endorses and complies with societal standards. The individual then volitionally abandons previously held deviant values. "Successful moral education seems to entail giving the deviant a sense of membership in a viable social group with an ideology, a ratio-

nale that explains the purpose of the group and his or her own life within it." (Hogan, 1993, p. 275)

It would seem that to make radical changes in value and character structure would require assisting the adolescent in joining or identifying with a socially compliant and attractive reference group. Examples of such groups might include the Police Athletic League, religious groups, or the Guardian Angels. When the group is perceived as valuable and relevant, but is indeed malevolent, we define it as a cult, and it can serve to remove the individual from societal norms rather than the reverse.

The teaching of values in the residential treatment facility will need to address the importance of obeying rules, respecting the property and rights of others, inhibiting aggressive behaviors, telling the truth, and negotiating conflicts regardless of the consequences. Teaching these values will need to be a joint effort of therapists and direct care workers who will serve both as disciplinarians and role models. Without such teaching, no amount of therapeutic intervention or behavior modification has a chance of generalizing beyond the confines of the program. If Hogan is correct in his reasoning, therapeutic efforts with adolescents in placement displaying antisocial behaviors and values may need to accept a broader social approach than is presently attempted at RTFs.

# Chapter 10

# Accessing Families

"You keep alluding to the importance of generalization of treatment to the home. That requires working with families."

"Our regulations require that the program be "family oriented" and that family reunification be the goal of placement. We try to involve all the families in family therapy or counseling and in the decision making and planning for their child. If that is not feasible, we must work with the referring agency to find a suitable replacement family."

"How many families actually get involved in such treatment?"

"About a third."

"Not such a good ratio."

"We have a problem. Many of our families are no longer intact, or they just lack the coping skills to deal with the child. If they were more competent as parents, we probably wouldn't have had to deal with the child to begin with."

"Aren't you making some value judgments here? The families you try to deal with are not successful, middle-class readers of *Parents* magazine and Dr. Spock. They raise their children as they were brought up. Who are you to label them dysfunctional because they don't attend PTA meetings?"

"Our regulations also require that we be 'culturally competent'—in other words, sensitive to and tolerant of the ethnic and cultural backgrounds of our families. It doesn't always work."

## DEFINING COUNSELING

Counseling may be defined as a structured relationship between a counselor and one or more people in which the goal is to effect positive changes in the functioning, adjustment, behavior, and happiness of the recipients. Family counseling assumes its own unique characteristics because the counselees already have a history and a relationship with one another. The counselor needs to assume a role as an objective and impartial observer of the manner in which family members relate to each other, to identify destructive patterns of interaction, and to facilitate more effective ways of functioning. When the family includes a child with severe emotional disturbance, the focus is more strongly directed to parental relationships with the disturbed child.

However, family counseling cannot be performed in a vacuum, and it is impossible and unreasonable to avoid addressing family issues that extend beyond the child's problem. Satir (1982) has pointed out the targeting that often occurs in families when the problems of one member are emphasized in order to disguise more general family dysfunctioning. It is not unusual to find that resolving the difficulties of the child targeted for counseling is followed by a crisis suddenly surfacing with another family member. Satir served as counselor for a twelve-year-old child with severe tension headaches. The successful treatment of the child using behavior therapy approaches was followed shortly after with the announced separation and later divorce of the parents.

There are numerous approaches to family counseling—dynamic, behavioral, cognitive, client centered, and transactional, to name a few. The differences among these approaches will not be covered here. Most approaches view the family as a system. A system is defined here as a complex interaction of all members of the family. The system both determines and is determined by all family members. The components of the system (family members) achieve a homeostatic equilibrium or balance which may or may not be effective but always serves some function. Satir (1982) assumes that dysfunctional communication is a central factor in family systems that do not work well. These ineffective communication patterns arise from the parents' own experiences in families and their unrealistic expectations of what they should receive from their current family members. Disappointments in meeting unrealistic expectations are accepted as evidence that they are unloved. The expectations are usually unspoken as are the rules under which a dysfunctional family operates. Typically, in such families, parents focus upon disruptive behaviors of the child. This focus diverts attention from their own communication difficulties. However, it serves temporarily to keep the family together and may bring them into therapy. A family therapist may serve to make the family aware of their unspoken feelings, disappointments, and rules of functioning. They can learn to see the child's behaviors as an expression of broader family problems.

Most residential treatment programs are not family oriented (Laufer, 1990). Despite the mandate of the Adoption Assistance and Child Welfare Act of 1980 (Public Law 96-272) that state service providers maintain a child with the family or make alternative permanent plans, if the parents cannot provide care, family involvement in residential treatment has often been minimal (Baker, Blacher, and Pfeiffer, 1993). Nor has family reunification been a primary goal (Allen and Pfeiffer, 1991). Baker and colleagues (1995) suggest that the reasons for this lack of family participation are threefold. Families may not be available to the child or may be so dysfunctional as to preclude participation. Reality constraints such as physical distance from the program or lack of financial resources may prevent incorporating the parents in treatment. Furthermore, treatment programs themselves may not value family participation and may not be equipped to develop such options for families. Treatment staff may view families in negative terms (e.g., as abusive) and may prefer that they remain uninvolved.

A survey of 267 staff members of three residential treatment centers for children administered by the Devereux Foundation (Baker et al., 1995) found that, while staff members were supportive on family involvement, it was more in the role of receiving help from staff than as active participants in the decision making regarding the child's program. Reunification with families was not strongly endorsed for the majority of children. Baker and colleagues recommend that agencies seeking greater family involvement will need to work with staff in promoting more positive attitudes about such involvement.

In Chapter 8, the perceptions of the child who has been physically or emotionally abused were discussed. Here, we will consider this situation from the perspective of the family and will end with what therapeutic interventions are dictated by these perceptions.

Family counseling in the RTF is often a frustrating and perhaps unsuccessful process. Families of the children referred have failed in some way as parents, since the child is now in placement. The families have been dysfunctional in many cases for long periods of time. Often only one parent remains in the family, with the absent member no longer identified as part of the family. It is not uncommon that children in an RFT have a parent in prison, often for instances of child abuse. Other families are disrupted by drug and alcohol problems or other ravages of poverty. Many of the parents who might have been available for counseling are poorly motivated to participate. The welfare system has relieved them of their responsibility to parent. Their own sense of worthlessness and helplessness precludes reassuming any responsibility. Many are angry at the child welfare agency that has taken their child and are not prepared to cooperate with the system. Yet, many parents do participate and work with the counselor to help the RTF bring about family reunification.

The natural family of a child in placement with either a foster family or at a residential treatment center has been unable to cope with the child and likely has a long history of family problems. Labeled dysfunctional by child welfare or juvenile justice professionals, natural families accept two cognitions despite their logical inconsistency. First, they are angry and resentful at the agency that has taken the child because of the implied accusation that they have been abusive, incompetent, and generally poor parents. They are also angry at the child for the misbehavior that led to the dissolution of the family. Second, they feel guilty because they too realize they have failed. The feeling of helplessness as parents compounds with the despair of poverty, addictions, marital problems, legal problems, psychiatric disturbance, or whatever other problems they are experiencing.

## STRUCTURING A COUNSELING RELATIONSHIP

Given these family concerns, it is a mistake to jump into a family counseling situation and expect the child or the parent to begin communicating at a high level of feeling. Similarly, even a problem-oriented counseling approach, in which parent and child contract with each other for certain quid pro quo behaviors, may be more than either party can carry out. We have learned by experience that it is best with traumatized children in placement to make few if any demands on either parent or child in the initial counseling situation. Initially, parents and children are asked to accept being with each other with a family counselor in a controlled situation. This contrived situation often serves as an in vivo desensitization of both parties to each other.

Neither party need talk very much except as meets the demands of the immediate task defined by the counselor. We find it best to begin by questioning about the situation that resulted in the child being placed. The counselor may be vocal, providing encouragement, praise, and reinforcement for the positive interactions that are transpiring. The counselor may also use this time, without taking away from the interactions between parent and child, to discuss the goals of the treatment, the philosophy and workings of the residential treatment program, and the objective of returning the child to a family situation as quickly as possible. This further defuses the anger either party may be experiencing about the placement which, the counselor emphasizes, will be short term. It is essential that the issue of leaving the program be addressed at the onset of counseling since family reunification is the goal of the program. Discharge planning thus becomes a primary objective of the counseling as well. The family should be questioned in turn as to what the perceived obstacles to discharge might be. This allows the family to deal directly with the reasons for placement and the issues that need to be addressed in counseling and in the program.

A secondary goal of the counseling will be to allow the parent to reestablish the parental role, taking cues from the child that he or she is ready to allow this to happen. One powerful strategy is to allow the parent time alone with the child doing something both will enjoy, such as going to the snack bar together or to an off-campus restaurant or movie. Staff may transport the family for these excursions but are not to act as escorts or in a supervisory capacity. The parent may need to be subsidized financially to accomplish these activities, but it is considered an essential part of the therapeutic process because of the empowerment it provides to the parent. The underlying principles here are to treat the parent with respect in their role as parent, while allowing the child some degree of control over this process by expressing preferences and the time when such interventions may occur.

It is only after such interventions that minimal limit setting, expectations, and demands may be imposed on the parent-child relationship. At this time, therapeutic leave, usually weekends at home, may be introduced. Goals for each therapeutic leave are set before the experience, and feedback about the success in achieving each goal is obtained when the child is brought back to the center. The duration of such home experiences is gradually increased as the child approaches discharge from the program. The success of these home experiences is given more significance than the behavior of the child at the residential treatment center. The failure of children at home, after being models of behavior at the treatment center, is a reality with children in such placement programs. Family preservation and reunification are elusive and often unaccomplished goals. Even after discharge, an active follow-up program of counseling is necessary to maintain progress.

Children are not "fixed" by any magical treatment program in isolation from their families. To expect this to happen is naive. Rather, treatment is a gradual process of reintroduction of the child to his or her family under controlled conditions and supervision. In some cases, we find that children adjust to the structure of the RTF but fail to make an appropriate adjustment at home. Families report that the most severe aggressive and destructive behaviors occur when the child comes for a home visit. For this reason, families sometimes resist inviting the child home. In some cases, when such visits are required by the funding agency, such as at the end of the academic year, families are faced with catastrophic situations. We were able to address this situation by the establishment of a facility on grounds that we refer to as the Family Training Center. A three-bedroom, ranch-style house has been renovated and furnished for this purpose with the help of a local foundation.

Families are invited to spend a weekend with their child at the facility and to engage in regular routines just as if they were at home. Staff are provided during this experience to observe, develop effective treatment plans, and make recommendations to the family. Many of the encounters are videotaped and used later in family counseling. Assignments are made, such as excursions to the food market or a local mall. Staff may or may not accompany the family during these experiences. A weekend with their family at the Family Training Center is a part of the tuition for all children enrolled in the RTF.

Therapists must learn to adapt available treatment models to their own particular tastes and style, as well as to the unique needs of the populations being served. What works for one therapist with middle-class, relatively well-educated families may not be well suited for families of a child welfare population of rebellious adolescents. We have found it necessary to modify traditional approaches to counseling and therapy to be effective with the diverse families of the children in the RTF.

## CHARACTERISTICS OF FAMILIES

First, some generalities about these families must be discussed. While we endorse the CASSP principles that mandate families be active participants in the treatment process and that they not be blamed for the child's problems, it is also necessary to recognize that these families may be handicapped in various ways:

- The families may live in geographic areas that are poverty-stricken, and the neighborhood and schools may be dangerous.
- Opportunities for social and recreational activities available for the child at the RTF may be unavailable for any of the family members at home.
- The family has been unable to provide for or cope with the child.
- Situations may have improved with the child in placement, but the added pressures of reunification may again tip the balance toward crisis.
- Families may manifest the same patterns of hopelessness and despair seen in the children.
- Families may show the same patterns of anger and aggressive response to problems as their child in placement.
- Families may distrust the social welfare system and professionals associated with the system because their child has been placed in the custody of others.

- They may expect to be treated with disrespect because they have lost respect for their own ability to cope.
- They may be overly sensitive to being rejected by the system and may perceive themselves to be mistreated when mistreatment did not occur and was not intended.
- They may not be appreciative of efforts to help them in counseling or therapy.

The problems that exist between the child and the parents may represent more than a breakdown in communication; they may represent serious attachment problems and failure to bond. Some families may therefore require extensive skill building in parenting, not just counseling.

### Establishing Goals

As in any form of family counseling, it is unrealistic to expect that counseling can be limited to any narrow goal. It is necessary to address any problems within the family in order to address return of the child to the home or to another setting. Family counseling with families of children in residential placement will cover housing, financial, social, and legal problems. They will be enmeshed in relationships of the family with the referring agency. This should come as no surprise to experienced family counselors but may arouse concerns about limit setting in program administrators.

The severity or intensity of the child's behavior as well as the severity of conditions at home may produce enormous resistance and skepticism in families to efforts to effect family reunification.

For these reasons, counselors and therapists need to be very cautious in accepting treatment goals that may be unrealistic for the child and the family and that may serve only to subject all parties to failure and unnecessary emotional pain. If family reunification is unrealistic, this fact needs to be accepted as early as possible in the treatment process and alternative plans formulated. Children can maintain effective relationships with their natural families even if they are living in foster homes or group home settings. Counseling can focus upon strengthening these relationships without the expectation of return to a home environment that cannot sustain them. The guilt that such an arrangement may arouse can be treated, and this is an acceptable treatment goal. Foster placement, made with the full participation of the natural family, may represent the least restrictive alternative for the child and be fully consistent with CASSP principles.

*   *   *

Treatment stories have no ending. Residential treatment does not provide cures. Perhaps the experience rubs off in affecting what happens next to the child. Certainly the ultimate criterion is what transpires after discharge. New referrals will replace old, and the process continues. Family counseling produces successes as well as outcomes that staff are not so proud to broadcast. RTFs continue to expand with federal wraparound funds fueling the referral streams. Family counseling can help an RTF avoid becoming just another way station in the child welfare placement process.

# Chapter 11

# Giving Medications

"How important are medications?"

"About half the children are receiving psychotropic medications regularly. The medications and their effects are reviewed once a month for each child."

"Do you really need them?"

"They can be very effective in certain situations, but they are probably misused too. Often psychiatrists prescribe antipsychotic meds to control nonspecific symptoms such as aggression which are not linked to any particular diagnosis. Many people believe this is poor medical practice. Some people call them 'chemical restraints.' Regulations require that such strong meds be reduced gradually after effective dosages are found. The intent is to substitute less intrusive and dangerous behavioral management for chemical management."

"So the psychiatrist calls the shots."

"Only for medications. Program administration and operations are handled by nonmedical staff. Staff work with the psychiatrist in formulating diagnoses and even in recommending meds. Some of our psychologists become pretty knowledgeable in psychopharmacology. Fiscal constraints limit the time psychiatrists can spend reviewing a case—usually no more than four cases an hour. That puts the burden on the staff to present information rapidly and efficiently."

"Still, it sounds like you run two programs—medical and psychosocial."

"It often is that way. We are trying to build bridges."

\* \* \*

About 1 percent of all school children and 6 to 8 percent of all students with handicaps are classified as seriously emotionally disturbed (Gadow, 1986). Of these, about 11 percent receive psychotropic medication for behavior disorders (Culliman, Gadow, and Epstein, 1987). This is probably an underestimate (Singh et. al., 1990) since it does not include the use of antiepileptic drugs, even when used to control behavioral disorder. A survey of teachers of socially and emotionally disturbed children in Illinois by Singh and colleagues (1990) indicates that teachers perceive the child's physician as the primary mover in placing a child on or removing the child from medications, with the school psychologist, parents, and the child's case committee playing a lesser contributory role. Teachers believe that they should be more involved in such decisions and that they should be receiving more training in the use of medications and the assessment of children placed on medications. Delusions, hallucinations, and hyperactivity are seen as the disorders most often leading to psychotropic medication in school children.

Curiously, depression was not listed as a disorder that frequently leads to prescription of psychotropics. Depending upon a number of factors, children enter one of the three child treatment systems. Those from more affluent families are likely to encounter the mental health system through child guidance clinics, private practitioners, or private psychiatric hospitals. Those from more disadvantaged families will likely encounter the child welfare system, unless they become adjudicated delinquent, in which case it will be the juvenile justice system. There are, then, three paradigms of management: treatment, placement, and punishment. Medication can be part of all three systems but is particularly associated with mental health.

## BACKGROUND

Prior to the development of the "major tranquilizers," mental illness was a more formidable entity than it is today. Mental hospitals were populated with large numbers of violent and unmanageable persons that made physical restraints, electroconvulsive shock, and even frontal lobotomies acceptable treatments. There is no question that the advent of Thorazine and other antipsychotics in the 1950s paved the way for massive deinstitutionalization and the creation of community programs. Today, the field of psychopharmacology has become enormously complex with classes of medications for the treatment not only of psychotic disorders but mood disorders and anxiety disorders as well. In addition, many medications originally intended for one purpose are now being used to treat behavioral problems with varying degrees of success. The use of psychotropics with children raises even more complex issues than their use with adults because of the immaturity of children, their developing nervous systems, and individual variations in response to drugs.

Furthermore, the area of pediatric psychopharmacology remains controversial because of human rights issues. Opponents of the use of such medication believe that their use is a basic violation of rights, designed to control behavior ("chemical restraints") for the convenience of parents, teachers, or society, not to help the child. This criticism is particularly pertinent to the use of certain drugs (e.g., lithium carbonate) to control aggressive behavior rather than to treat a known or presumed biological dysfunction. Supporters of such medications insist that serious conditions such as depression and schizophrenia represent biological imbalances and must be treated chemically. Hodapp and Dykens (1994) have referred to the large discrepancy between psychological/educational and medical approaches to mental retardation as dual cultures. They point out that practitioners of the two approaches have failed to establish meaningful communication. Those with a medical or biological bias place little confidence in psychological or learning mechanisms, while psychologists and educators are often oblivious to biological and genetic determinants. A similar situation exists in the treatment of emotionally disturbed children, except that three cultures—mental health, child welfare, and juvenile justice—may be involved. The issue of psychotropic medication clearly reflects this cultural disparity.

## BIOLOGICAL BASES OF BEHAVIOR

Not all behavior manifest in emotional disturbance is functional and subject to control by environmental manipulations. Some behavior is biologically driven or at least biologically influenced and not easily changed by psychosocial intervention. Genetic and neurological influences upon behavior interact in complex ways with environmental factors. Many drugs used for altering moods and behavior operate upon the synaptic level of the nervous system. Neurons, the basic units of the nervous system, do not connect directly with each other at the synaptic junction. A slight gap, or synapse, is bridged by a chemical process. These chemicals, labeled neurotransmitters, may exert an excitatory or inhibitory action from the sending to the receiving neuron. A number of neurotransmitters have been identified, including acetylcholine, serotonin, norepinephrine, and dopamine. It is these chemicals that are targeted by drugs used to combat many manifestations of emotional disturbance. Some drugs prevent the release of the neurotransmitter; others occupy the receptor site of the neuron so that reuptake of the neurotransmitter is blocked. Opiates and psychedelic drugs are also believed to affect mental functioning by acting upon neurotransmitters, often producing schizophrenic-like states.

Antianxiety drugs such as diazepam (Valium) depress the action of the nervous system. Antipsychotic drugs such as chlorpromazine (Thorazine) belong to a family of drugs called phenothiazines. These appear to act by occupying the postsynaptic receptors of dopamine neurons, preventing the neurons from firing. One theory of schizophrenia professes that it is caused by an excessive level of dopamine in the reticular system of the brain. In contrast, dopamine is thought to be depleted in Parkinson's Syndrome. For this reason, the overuse of antipsychotics may produce masklike Parkinsonian features such as tremors and facial rigidity. Antipsychotics were once referred to as major tranquilizers, but this was a misnomer and has been dropped.

Some antidepressant drugs elevate the mood of depressed individuals, energizing rather than tranquilizing. They act by increasing the availability of two neurotransmitters, norepinephrine and serotonin. Two major classes of antidepressants accomplish this in different ways. The monoamine oxidase (MAO) inhibitors block the activity of an enzyme that destroys both norepinephrine and serotonin, thus increasing their concentration in the brain. The tricyclic antidepressants prevent the reuptake of the two neurotransmitters, thus prolonging the duration of their action.

## CLASSES OF MEDICATIONS

The term "psychotropic medication" refers to any of the drugs that are used to affect mental functioning. The term "neuroleptic" refers to those psychotropics used to control psychotic disorders affecting thinking, perception, and behavior. Antipsychotic drugs include Haldol, Clozaril, Mellaril, Thorazine, Risperdal, and many others. (Trade names rather than generic medication names are used here.)

Medications geared specifically toward reducing anxiety include Ativan, BuSpar, Halcion, Klonopin, Valium, Librium, and others. These drugs were at one time labeled minor tranquilizers.

Drugs used to reduce manic symptoms include lithium carbonate and are used in bipolar disorders. Antidepressant medications include such drugs as Elavil, Tofranil, Prozac, Paxil, and Zoloft. Certain stimulants such as Cylert, Dexedrine, and Ritalin are effective with ADHD symptoms. Anticonvulsant medications include Tegretol, Dilantin, and Depakote. Some anticonvulsants are also used as mood stabilizers. Some medications such as Cogentin are used to prevent Parkinsonian symptoms. These are generally cholinergic medications.

Finally, there are nonpsychiatric medications such as Inderal and Catapres that affect the adrenergic arousal system and may affect conditions such as Intermittent Explosive Disorder involving overarousal.

### Application

"Med reviews" at one RTF are held once a month in each building. The psychiatrist meets with the clinical director, case managers, and other members of the team to review the medications of every child receiving psychotropic drug treatments. The clinical director or psychologist indicates the current medication and dosage; the team reviews the child's behavior over the past month; the psychiatrist dictates any medication changes deemed necessary. The nurse makes note of these changes for the chart and is responsible for communicating the changes to the primary physician who writes the prescription. Sometimes there is a time lag before the change actually takes place because of transmittal time to the pharmacy. These procedures are elaborately detailed in the procedures manual of the RTF. This process has been forced to become more efficient since the opening of the first building. With only a few children to treat, the psychiatrist was able to spend several hours listening to staff describe many aspects of the child's history and current life circumstances. As the number of children increased and quality assurance was added to the program, discussions had to be curtailed and were limited primarily to current behaviors. Because of the hourly cost of the psychiatrist and certain limitations in the allowable costs for medical assistance billing, it was necessary to streamline the process so that at least four children could be reviewed every hour. Separate team meetings were held weekly to discuss the children clinically, but the psychiatrist does not attend these meetings. Medical assistance pays only for face-to-face contacts between the psychiatrist and the child.

Many children do well with certain medications. Children diagnosed with Attention Deficit Hyperactivity Disorder show increased attention span and may do better in school with stimulants such as Ritalin or Dexedrine. Others show no response to these drugs. We have seen situations in which children who are heavily medicated show marked improvements when they are taken off the medications entirely. Many children do well with a combination of psychological therapies, family involvement, and medication.

## CRITICISM

All too often there is a discontinuity between the medical and the psychosocial treatment. What is needed is a unified multimodal treatment model with both components of treatment working in concert, rather than having two distinct and sometimes contradictory approaches.

Numerous criticisms have been leveled at the use of psychoactive drugs or at least at the abuse of such approaches. The appropriate utilization of drug therapies presumes an accurate diagnosis be made so that the medication can precisely target a biological disorder. The reliability of psychiatric diagnosis has been seriously questioned, particularly in children and in complex situations as, for example, when there are dual diagnoses of emotional disturbance and mental retardation. Psychoactive drugs often have serious side effects, and overmedication can cause irreversible damage and even death. Tardive dyskinesia is a muscular disorder affecting involuntary movements of the mouth and chin associated with overmedication using antipsychotic drugs. Reaction against the use of "cruel and unusual" punishment to residents of mental hospitals or institutions for persons with mental retardation led to an equal concern about the use of psychotropic medications. Psychoactive drugs are used in various ways by physicians. In many instances, powerful medications designed for one purpose have proven useful for another. Certain medications, for example, which are commonly used to prevent seizures, may have applications in controlling mood states. Lithium, a treatment of choice for bipolar (manic depressive) disorder is often used to control aggressive behavior. In addition to maintaining therapeutic blood levels, these drugs are often given on an as-needed basis to quell an aggressive or destructive episode. These are referred to as "PRNs" (*pro re naia*) by medical staff, signifying an as-needed use. PRNs have been targeted as chemical restraints, particularly repugnant to those concerned with the human rights of persons with mental handicaps. Additionally, the use of drugs to control mood or behavior does not address psychological, family, or social factors affecting the behavior. Faulty attitudes or methods of coping, learned over a lifetime, cannot be changed solely by the use of medication. There are no medications to cure the pain of abuse or abandonment. Ritalin will not find Robert a family or relieve Ramona's anger.

Another critical issue is the effectiveness of medications as compared with psychological approaches or no treatment at all. Appropriate research designs exist for assessing drug actions. These involve the use of control groups and double-blind procedures in which neither the person receiving the drug nor the person administering it is aware of whether the drug or a placebo is being given. Unfortunately, in many cases the drugs commonly used with disturbed children have not been properly evaluated for the specific type of condition for which they are being prescribed. Drug evaluation studies often are subjective and poorly controlled. A well-known psychiatric consultant in Pennsylvania (Weisblatt, 1994), for example, is critical of the overdiagnosis of psychotic disorders in children with mental health and mental retardation symptoms resulting in the prescribing of antipsychotics in such cases. His thesis is that such children have mood disorders that should be treated with drugs specific to those conditions. Sovner and Weisblatt (1992) have criticized the overuse of the term psychotic to be synonymous with schizophrenia, suggesting that "psychosis" as a label refers only to the severity of a major mental illness and not a diagnosis. They believe that antipsychotic medications should be used to treat specific psychiatric diagnoses and not to treat behaviors such as aggression that are not specific to any particular diagnosis.

## EFFECTIVENESS OF PSYCHOTROPICS WITH CHILDREN

Eighteen years ago, a review of psychopharmacological intervention with emotionally disturbed children and adolescents (Wilson and Sherrets, 1979) lamented that literature available at the time was sparse and insufficient to draw empirical conclusions about drug efficacy. Referring largely to subjective, anecdotal reports, Wilson and Sherrets saw promise in the use of medications in four areas: epilepsy, childhood schizophrenia and autism, "minimal brain dysfunction" (now referred to as ADHD), and (curiously) enuresis. They recognized that "no child should be subjected to behavior medication solely as a means of behavior control, or certainly not without a thorough evaluation of the child and his environment" (Wilson and Sherrets, 1979, p. 64). They also recognized that medication use should not be undertaken independently but in conjunction with teachers and other professionals in order to maximize the likelihood of success.

By 1993, the situation had improved somewhat, but with the exception of the use of methylphenidate (Ritalin) for ADHD, controlled studies of the efficacy of psychotropics are still sparse. Although medical practice had accepted the use of these drugs, justification was largely on the basis of results with adults. A detailed review by Greenhill and Setterberg (1993) notes the significant increase in the prevalence of major psychiatric disorders in adolescents as compared with younger children. Difficulties in diagnosing the emerging of first episodes of disorders in adolescence, the need to involve families in the assessment process, and problems in enforcing compliance with medication regimens contribute to the complexity of the problem.

Although adolescent depressive disorders may appear identical to those seen in adults, there are too few controlled studies to demonstrate that antidepressants are superior to placebos in effectiveness in treating depression. Furthermore, there is a risk of antidepressant-induced mania or hypomania as well as suicidal preoccupations (specifically with Prozac*). There is some evidence that mood stabilizers such as lithium are superior to placebos in the control of explosive aggression.

The situation with anxiety-reducing drugs is equally murky. "Although the anxiety disorders in adults have been investigated carefully and have shown symptom responsiveness in controlled studies, similar large controlled outpatient studies in childhood and adolescence have yet to be carried out" (Greenhill and Setterberg, 1993, p. 802).

Again, the use of neuroleptics in childhood schizophrenia is based largely on research with adults. Neuroleptics show promise for effective treatment of the primary symptoms of schizophrenia (delusions, hallucinations, thinking disorder, bizarre behavior) as well as for nonschizophrenic psychotic symptoms but do not appear useful with secondary schizophrenic symptoms (poverty of speech, flat affect, withdrawal, apathy).

ADHD may be the most referred condition for psychotropic medication. Greenhill and Setterberg estimate that between 2 percent and 2.5 percent of elementary school children have been placed on medication to reduce the symptoms of ADHD. There is extensive literature dealing with short-term (four to twelve weeks) studies of children treated medically for this condition. Although children continue to meet psychiatric criteria through age fifteen, there are no long-term studies tracking children from primary school through high school. The medication (stimulants) appears to

---

*In February 1990, a study published in the *American Journal of Psychiatry* reported that sixteen patients being treated with Prozac became increasingly aware of self-destructive tendencies. Although this finding has been discredited by others within the medical community, the issue remains unsettling (Teicher, 1990). King (1991) has reported similar findings in children.

work equally well at all age levels, and there is no evidence that it leads to the later use of illegal stimulants. Controlled studies suggest significant improvement in attention and decreased hyperactivity, making the child more amenable to learning in school.

The use of psychotropics, including neuroleptics, has not abated, despite its critics. Within residential treatment facilities psychotropics are increasingly monitored, with mandates for medication reductions to minimal levels. The future of these drugs appears positive for disorders involving clear biological conditions, such as ADHD, mood disorders, and schizophrenia, but less clear for behavior and conduct disorders in which the biological links are uncertain.

# Chapter 12

# Building for the Future—
# Wanted: A Blueprint for Change

"So where does the program go now?"

"It expands. We have no choice. The program makes money when the beds are filled. We will soon have seventy-two beds. Most of the beds will be for dually diagnosed children. The change will serve to recenter us in the direction from which we came—mental retardation."

"What's managed care going to do to you?"

"Who knows? Less revenues, greater accountability. There will probably be greater requirements for credentialing of staff, so more professionalization. I don't think that's bad. Our facility will survive managed care just as it survived other changes over the years."

"Can you maintain quality programming and still get bigger?"

"I worry about that. It's not just that we'll need more staff. There's a critical mass that taxes administration, support services, and the clinicians. Economies of scale prevail, and clinical expertise does not expand as fast as the census."

"And what about you? How much longer are you going to be doing this kind of work?"

"I think I'll hang around a little while longer. I want to see how it all plays out."

"So how are you going to improve things?"

"I am going to try to apply an intervention model based on what I think these kids need to learn and haven't."

"You have a theory?"

"It's premature for theories. Other workers have proposed some basic values children need to learn to become socialized. I would try to build on those."

"You're going to cure behavior disorder?"

"There are no magic cures. I'm going to try to develop a positive approach based on what all children should learn, not just disturbed children. Then I will need to persuade some people that it ought to be tried. Then the approach should be evaluated."

"Sounds like a lifetime of work. You don't have that long, my friend."

"Perhaps enough time to get started and have others pick up the ball."

## RECAPITULATION

In this volume, an attempt has been made to provide some conceptual background for residential treatment facilities for emotionally disturbed adolescents and to chronicle the experience of one facility in establishing such a program. Our efforts are not offered as a model of treatment but rather as an honest depiction of what RTFs are all about.

RTFs did not spring up in a vacuum but evolved from roots embedded in the soil of child welfare, child development, special education, psychology, social work, and child psychiatry disciplines. They are one option among many, past and current, including orphanages, institutions, foster care, juvenile detention centers, child guidance clinics, and psychiatric hospitals. The issues involved range from genetics through a variety of approaches to training, discipline, education, counseling, and psychotherapy. From colonial times until the present, social planners have wrestled with how to cope with our city's problems of blight and poverty, not the least of which is that of the unwanted children of dysfunctional homes. No one solution has had universal effectiveness. Today massive governmental agencies, child and family advocacy groups, and professionals still grope to provide the requisite protective and treatment services for over a half-million children in placement. Although good programs exist, the Oliver Twists of previous centuries are still with us. The final word in this book is an attempt at evaluation and a guess at the future.

After three years of intimate involvement with an RTF, with experience in both the operations and administrative realms, we have some perspective in understanding what we have been doing. Basic questions about the utility and efficacy of this effort are still largely unresolved. Empirical outcome studies evaluating the program or its components have not been performed. The specter of managed care, relentlessly overshadowing us, will force the addition of quality assessment procedures that will accomplish that goal. For the moment, the impressions provided here are entirely subjective and untested.

The most basic question concerns the value of the RTF. Do we provide a service to troubled children by sequestering them from their family and community in group settings with children who share many of the same backgrounds, problems, and problem behaviors as themselves? Perhaps that question is far too broad and unanswerable in the abstract. A more meaningful approach may be to define the conditions under which referral to an RTF might be justified in comparison with other possible referral options. The conditions suggested below do not address the structure of the treatment program but assume that a meaningful experience can be provided.

The most serious criticism of the RTF may be that, in practice, the children referred are not being sent because of a proven track record with that specific type of child or problem. Children are referred because all previous placements have failed. The RTF is often not a treatment of choice but a treatment of last resort. There is, therefore, a selection bias. Only the most difficult problems will find their way to the RTF and for the wrong reasons. Within those parameters, it is essential to find out what the RTF does well. Any particular setting must learn to identify its specific expertise and then to hone that approach to make it a specialization. The treatment should have a specific concept or philosophy that provides a common thread running through all program components and that is different from other programs. Once such a philosophy has been developed, it will affect the selection of children, nature of treatment, and discharge planning. RTFs do not "fix" children. Those with emotional disturbance will continue to manifest emotional problems. The RTF can, on the other hand, arrive at a meaningful diagnosis, initiate a stabilizing medication regimen, and identify a set of family, school, and community supports that will facilitate a successful discharge.

It seems self-evident that referral to a group-living treatment facility may be justified when less restrictive settings, such as the natural family, foster family placement, or group homes, are not available. In some cases, a less restrictive setting may become available in the future. Behavioral changes in the child are required to make the less restrictive setting more feasible, or work is required to prepare the family to receive the child or to develop a suitable discharge plan.

Another potential use is as a step down from more restrictive psychiatric hospitalization or as an alternative to hospitalization. This presumes that effective treatment of serious emotional problems is available at the RTF, while the greater structure and security of a hospital setting is no longer required. With conditions of depression or psychosis, a greater degree of risk is assumed by the RTF. In these cases, the RTF can provide needed stabilization of the child in the form of medication adjustment, behavior management, and support to allow further step-down programming. The RTF can assess the child's needs and strengths and identify community and family supports necessary for family reunification.

The grouping of aggressive children together in the same facility may be the most pernicious aspect of the RTF. As stated earlier, children who learn violence at an early age view aggressive behavior as an acceptable, useful, and potentially rewarding way of life. Even if staff are successful in modeling more appropriate strategies for resolving conflict, a congregate residential living facility for a group of children similarly inclined provides ample opportunity for confirmation of this belief. Psychotherapy stressing cognitive restructuring and a therapeutic milieu emphasizing prosocial values are suggested in this book as intervention approaches. It may be that for such an approach to work, children must be treated at an early age—perhaps at an age traditionally not used for residential care. This line of reasoning lends credibility to involving families in treatment as early as possible for children showing signs of oppositional behavior. It also suggests the use of foster placements or therapeutic foster family care when the natural family is not a viable resource.

The decision to operate a residential treatment facility with emotionally disturbed adolescents brings with it a risk-management situation of enormous proportions. No matter how structured the program and how sophisticated the therapies, children are going to be placed in jeopardy. Staff may act in ways that hurt, not help. Much of the behavior that occurs will be blamed upon the emotional problems of the children. Often unrecognized is the fact that the milieu itself can create problems. The children do not want to be in a group setting with other disturbed children. They want to be with their families. They want the same stability and advantages as other children. They are serious students of TV, and they buy the American dream just as any other child. The interactions among eight or ten or sixteen seriously disturbed, aggressive, or victimized children are not therapeutic. A social structure emerges with leaders and followers and a complex set of rules. The goals imposed by clinicians and program planners may be relatively inconsequential compared with the operating principles of the gang culture that develops. Children will learn to survive the experience that we may describe as therapeutic but which may for any specific child be rigid compliance with powerful and sometimes malevolent forces. It does not have to be this way.

Program planners and implementers need to be aware that all is not therapeutic just because we wish it to be. For some children, residential living may be survival through compliance with demands of other children that are anything but therapeutic. We believe these instances are the exception, not the rule, but they do occur.

Even a positive milieu can have an unanticipated negative effect. At one RTF, the program budget includes money for parties, gifts, community trips, and other extras. Many of the children have volunteers who buy them presents, invite them home for dinner, and take them to special events and activities. Critics have suggested that we, as professional caregivers, are unnecessarily tantalizing them, for when they leave they can have none of these advantages. We are, it is pointed out, setting them up to expect and desire luxuries that their natural environments cannot provide. In such cases, the program is unrealistic and perhaps cruel. We defend the program by pointing out that we want the children to learn new experiences and options and to have goals to which they can aspire. Perhaps the answer is to provide the experiences but also counsel them in ways which will make them realize that such advantages are not easily acquired and may not be immediately available to them when they return home. There are no easy answers here.

Once the child is admitted, a viable discharge plan should be formulated. Indeed, such planning should begin prior to admission. Since the goal of most RTF programs is family reunification and community reintegration, every aspect of the program should be designed as a step toward discharge. A tentative discharge date should be formulated and presented to the child, his or her family, and the referring agency upon admission. Treatment goals must be realistic in relation to discharge plans. An effective plan for involving families in the treatment and discharge process must be formulated and implemented. If it should become clear that this plan has little chance of success, alternative plans should be made as early as possible in the treatment process.

This book has described various components of the treatment process at one RTF. One key issue in the implementation of the program has been the attainment of a realistic balance among administrative, regulatory, and clinical perspectives. Licensing monitors and inspectors repeatedly remind us that regulations provide a minimal standard of program quality; they should not be accepted as the program itself. Each facility will impose its own treatment "spin," depending upon the perceived needs of the children and the orientation of the clinical director. In practice, it becomes extremely difficult for a clinical director to superimpose the best practice, theoretical, or conceptual standards while also being responsible for maintaining documentation, planning interagency and intraagency staff meetings, preparing for licensing inspections, developing individualized "strength-based" treatment goals, and directing ongoing individual, group, and family therapies. When fiscal managers require that beds not remain empty, criteria for admission to the program are often abandoned. Decisions to accept only those children who have a family who will become active in the treatment and discharge process become too easily compromised in the face of administrative pressure. We believe it best to develop a table of organization with an administrative director responsible for the fiscal and regulatory aspects of the program, yet supportive of the clinical treatment model as well.

Provision of appropriate education in the least restrictive setting also becomes an administrative and often a political issue. Our facility has a tradition of providing special education at an on-site school. Yet, our regulators cautioned us that the newer referrals came to us because of behavioral and emotional problems and should be attending school in a community setting. Arrangements to refer these children to the local school district met with firm resistance from the local school authorities. Although mandated by law to accept the children, school authorities made it clear that there was community and board resistance to accepting "delinquent," inner-city children into their suburban setting. Again, fiscal reasons may have been the key deterrent. Although the child's home school district was required to pay their tuition, it was often at a rate far below the suburban school's regular charge. Gradually, we made gains until the majority of children were being educated off campus. Those children who did have learning problems and could be kept in the more restrictive special education facility also presented difficulties. Education staff developed a therapeutic learning program. When their teachers seemed more interested in counseling the children than educating them in a traditional manner, we became alarmed. The children also complained that it wasn't a real school. Eventually, a balance was reached, but the achievement of a unified school and residential program is an elusive goal and one that we have not yet accomplished.

It is essential that an RTF have a network of referral resources to serve as an exit for children. Ideally, the RTF should be administratively responsible for its own step-down programs such as foster family care, therapeutic foster homes, and group homes. In this way, there can be continuity and follow-up with therapeutic goals established during the child's stay at the RTF.

The provision of a safe environment for child management is directly related to issues of selection of residents and training of staff. Facilities need to realistically assess their own capabilities. Difficult behaviors require staff competent to handle them. If a facility is not prepared to deal with suicidal gestures or sexual acting out or drugs, then these behaviors, occurring with consistency in children, should be a red flag precluding admission. To do otherwise, is unethical and exposes both the child and the facility to risk. We regard the admission procedure as a high priority and hope to develop a procedure for selection—perhaps a risk scale—that will increase the likelihood of successful outcomes by closing the door to children we have no capability of treating.

Training is a critical need for staff. Yet, as Shealy (1995) observes, more than skills and knowledge are required. The RTF will be superior to the child's home environment only if there are staff capable and willing to form emotional bonds and trusting relationships with children—such qualities transcend training, requiring a sophisticated selection procedure for hiring. The realities of budgetary restraints make this extremely difficult.

In elaborating these ideas, we draw from a literature that is more than 100 years old. We are not the first to wrestle with the tangled weeds that have choked normal development in abused and abandoned children. But, we are able to draw upon the experience of dealing with a small group of challenging youngsters who have allowed us neither to relax our vigilance nor fail to appreciate the complexity of their problems.

Perhaps first in importance in the following formulation is the conviction that each child carries with him or her a basic will to preserve his or her own integrity. No matter how serious the diagnosis, no matter how extreme the behavior pattern, the child maintains an inner resilience that guards him or her from further trauma. It is this strength that both frustrates and assists us in treatment. A history of physical and emotional abuse or of insult to their basic biological infrastructure engenders the most primitive fight-or-flight reaction. At all cost, the child must preserve that sense of self that is his or her identity. When bonding with the primary significant others—the parents—has been severely interfered with, the child will erect a barrier of distrust and defensive vigilance that may never be totally penetrated. All adults become potential adversaries. Distinguishing between those who profess to care or to want to help from those who have violated his or her trust may become an impossible task. This impenetrable barrier will sabotage the efforts of the most skillful therapist, despite the beneficence of the most nurturing of caretakers or the benefit of the most beautiful of environments. Yet, this need to preserve the ego from further assault or even annihilation also provides the strength for the child to continue fighting. Curiously, it is often the other children in the program who provide the opening wedge.

The child will trust his or her peers when it is perceived that they too have been assaulted, that they too are vulnerable. It is for this reason that the subculture, emphasized by Polsky (1962), assumes so much importance. And once this process begins, the child may grow to realize that others can be allowed entrance to the inner circle of self and feelings he or she has strived so hard to protect.

## DEFINING TREATMENT

It seems self-evident that residential treatment settings should provide active treatment, but there have been no reports of the extent to which such settings, many now funded at least partially by medical assistance (wraparound) dollars, actually do. Although regulations at the federal and state level specify minimum standards of care, they do not adequately define what constitutes treatment. This chapter, written from the perspective of a clinician and trainer in an RTF, attempts to provide some guidelines.

### What Are the Parameters of Treatment?

The definition of psychological treatment implies change in personality or emotional structure in a manner that impacts favorably upon behavior, adjustment, happiness, and productivity. It further implies a technology that, properly applied, effects results which should be demonstrable by objective means of measurement and should be apparent as well to the recipient of treatment. Treatment requires, then, a giver and a receiver as well as a setting identified as a place where treatment is applied. In the broadest sense, treatment refers to a complex process that can involve positive interpersonal interactions, learning experiences, and the opportunity for self-examination and insight. It may target more than one individual as the recipient, as in the case of family or group treatment. In the case of a residential treatment facility, the term treatment refers to a broad range of services, interactions, and settings, all presumably designed to accomplish roughly the same goals.

### What Does This Definition Presume?

Treatment is based upon a number of explicit and implicit presumptions regarding process and implementation:

- There are identifiable goals for improvement.
- There are objective criteria for operationalizing these goals.
- The behaviors specified as goals are changeable.
- The treatment agency has relevant technology to change these behaviors, and the staff are competent, sufficiently trained, and motivated to apply this technology.
- All components of the treatment program are consistent and sufficiently integrated to accomplish the same treatment goals.
- The persons referred to the agency have problems compatible with the treatment resources of the treatment agency.
- The target of the treatment is the appropriate locus of the problem requiring treatment.
- There are procedures in place to consistently evaluate the effectiveness of treatment for each individual and for the agency as a whole.
- There is an identifiable beginning and end to treatment according to measurable criteria.
- Once treatment reaches an end in terms of such criteria, the individual will be discharged from the program to a suitable setting.

### Failure to Provide Treatment

These presumptions would seem to be minimal for an agency to define itself as a treatment facility. When anticipated benefits of treatment are not forthcoming, it is likely to be on the basis of one or more of these presumptions being faulty.

Perhaps one of the most frequent reasons for treatment failure is identification of the wrong target for treatment or, more often, omission of one or more critical targets. For instance, failure to involve the family in a treatment program for the child when the purpose of the program is family reunification is such a case.

Another reason for failure is the acceptance of children whose problems are not a good match with the capabilities of the facility. An example would be admitting a psychotic child when staff have no training or experience in dealing with this type of behavior.

A third reason for failure is the absence of an adequate treatment approach relevant to the problem. This can occur because of inadequate assessment of the child's problem (e.g., functional analysis of symptoms), poorly trained staff, behaviors resistant to treatment, absence of client motivation for treatment, or social, family, or community factors determining behavior that are so powerful they are prepotent over any changes effected by treatment. Polsky (1962), describing the effect of the social milieu in a residential treatment facility for delinquent adolescents, observed that the peer culture was far more powerful than staff therapists in determining behavior. Therapists themselves were too far removed from the residents to deal with day-to-day issues in any meaningful fashion. Pelton (1989, 1991) has been a longtime critic of the social welfare system for turning social workers into police rather than helping agents. The real issue is poverty, he charges, not dysfunctional families.

Additional reasons for the absence of treatment can be both administrative and economic. One deterrent may be the degree of perceived risk in providing treatment. Children might be seen as too "psychologically fragile" to manage in other than purely supportive ways. Treatment approaches may be viewed as dangerous in other than a locked and well-controlled psychiatric setting. The treatment of fire setters or sexual offenders are examples. Finally, treatment is costly in terms of a competent therapist's time. Many facilities that advertise themselves as treatment settings are poorly staffed with senior-level clinicians.

## What Are Realistic Goals of Treatment?

Earlier concepts of residential treatment seemed to embrace a simplistic notion that problems were centered primarily in the child and that treatment, properly applied in out-of-home settings, would "fix" whatever was wrong and return the child to his or her family. Most clinicians today would take a more realistic, less ambitious view of their role. Rather than fixing a broken child, treatment can provide a respite for the child and the family at a critical period, can identify strengths and weaknesses in the family, and can prescribe necessary supports for the family after the child returns home. Programs are being asked under managed care guidelines to provide this service in shorter and shorter periods of time, with rapid turnover of clients. Treatment programs are going to need to accommodate to this task to survive in a competitive market, becoming more effective and more efficient in the treatment process.

## What Are the Risks of Treatment?

All treatment involves risks. There is the risk of failure after raising the expectations of the child, family, agency, and staff that the child will return home or at least improve sufficiently to live in a less restrictive setting. Such failures may merely add another way station to a long sequence of ineffective out-of-home placements for the child, exacerbating the defeatist attitude of the child and the anger and frustration of the family. The risk to the referring agency and the treatment facility are minimal. There are always more children. Agencies are accustomed to failure perhaps because real treatment is relatively rare.

The reaction of staff to failure may be more intense. Staff working with emotionally disturbed children often invest a great deal emotionally in such children. Staff burnout takes many forms. It is not uncommon to observe staff expressing resentment when a child with whom they have formed an attachment returns home to a situation they know is less than adequate. More devastating to staff are situations in which a child who was seemingly placing his or her life in order suddenly regresses to earlier antisocial patterns. The development of "messiah" complexes by therapists with regard to persons they treat is a well-known occupational hazard.

A risk to all residential treatment is the uncertainty of generalization of any real changes that might occur in the child while in residential treatment once he or she returns home. Conditions operative within the controlled residential setting can never be completely duplicated in the home. Behavior modification efforts within the RTF (e.g., levels systems) may serve to make good citizens of children while in treatment but are more difficult to replicate at home. One parent of a child in residential treatment complained that the program had ruined her child by providing luxuries and advantages that she could not afford to provide at home. Her child actually resisted discharge efforts for many months for this reason. Consequently, it is essential that families be included in treatment and that follow-up supports be provided after reunification.

## How Should Therapists Be Trained?

Therapists in RTFs are often beginning psychologists and social workers without extensive course work or supervised internship experiences. Because of the intensity of disruptive behaviors in such settings, they may be thrown into the most challenging situations with severely disturbed children and families. Economic considerations, especially under managed care guidelines, may preclude having more experienced staff working with children in treatment or even proper supervision of child care workers in therapeutic interventions. Some treatment settings may limit treatment to behavior modification approaches, perhaps translated solely into a level system.

Whether the approach is behavioral or more traditional therapeutic intervention, children deserve competent treatment. It is essential that treatment staff maintain open communication and training opportunities through regular team meetings, case presentations, workshops, symposia, and other training opportunities. Even experienced clinicians require opportunities for discussing cases and approaches with mentors and colleagues.

It is easy for residential treatment to deteriorate to little more than temporary custodial care. It is not so easy to maintain the RTF as a treatment setting. Treatment in the RTF, as in any clinical setting, needs to be closely tied to theoretical formulation, developmental level, diagnosis, and presenting problems. If staff arrive unprepared for this challenge, internal training is essential.

It would seem self-evident that frequent and regular staff training meetings for formal presentations of theory and technique, case presentations, monitoring of therapies, and mutual feedback from mentors and colleagues is a requisite of any treatment program.

### The Challenge

Treatment defined according to the criteria elaborated above remains an elusive and ambitious ideal within the realities of contemporary treatment settings. Clinicians need to advocate for competent evaluation and treatment programs, consistent with their training and the principles of their disciplines, despite pressures to fill beds, maintain a balanced budget, and negotiate the hazards of managed care. To do less is unethical. Now, more than ever, the danger of losing the treatment within residential treatment facilities confronts us.

## THE NEED FOR A CONCEPTUAL MODEL

The most outstanding need for the RTF is a unifying conceptual model that derives logically from the characteristics of the target population. By a conceptual model, I refer to an underlying framework for treatment that provides structure to all aspects of the treatment program—therapies, staff training, residential milieu, and education. The clinical literature offers a wealth of models and associated treatment strategies consistent with specific models. Although the need for such an approach seems self-evident, I suggest that it may not exist or be sufficiently pursued in many cases.

I see at least two advantages of a conceptual model. First, and most obvious, is the need to unify various, diverse staff members representing many professional disciplines in order to establish a seamless, consistent program. Residential living and education, for example, should not be separate programs but integrated arms of a homogeneous program working toward similar treatment and learning goals.

Second, a conceptual model allows for meaningful and significant distinctions among RTFs. There is supportive evidence establishing the efficacy of several treatment approaches with emotionally disturbed adolescents but not a great deal of evidence to endorse one approach over another. Treatment models and strategies used by therapists depend largely on their own training and prejudices. By identifying itself as a center using behavioral-support approaches, for example, an RTF allows referring agencies to make more intelligent referrals for specific types of problems. The RTF gains expertise by focusing its efforts conceptually and may attract graduate students seeking training in specific treatment modalities.

### Prerequisites of Such a Model

Apart from the conceptual approach, the model should conform with certain "givens" deriving from regulations and CASSP principles. Treatment should be targeted toward placement in less restrictive settings, preferably the natural family. Treatment should address the developmental needs and emotional characteristics of the target populations, be strength based, and sufficiently operational to guide the structuring of assessment, intervention, and program evaluation efforts. Treatment should be theoretically sound, empirically based, and regularly evaluated and modified based upon empirical evaluations of process and outcome variables. Treatment should be realistic. Short-term treatment at an RTF is not going to provide a "fix" but rather some tools, skills, coping strategies, and supports for both the adolescent and the family.

In Chapter 8, I have already suggested a cognitive model as a basis for psychotherapy. Other chapters have indicated the need to involve families in treatment and have indicated that the characteristics of the targeted population include their adolescent development, behavioral diagnoses, histories of separation and disruptions in attachment to natural families, and histories of being witness to and victims of violence and abuse. I end this book by referring to a treatment model that offers promise but that needs to be operationalized more than its authors have done. The model was developed by Brendtro, Brokenleg, and Van Bockern (1990) and translates easily into the treatment goals and service plan for each child.

We assume that every child has basic needs for safety and protection, nurturance, environmental stimulation, and acceptance and love by positive role models. In most cases, these needs are met by a family and extended family. For some children, these needs are thwarted early in life. Instead of nurturance and affection, they receive abuse, neglect, and in extreme cases, abandonment. Their role models may be unable or unwilling to meet these needs or they may be absent entirely. The result emotionally for the child is alienation, chronic vigilance and distrust, anger, helplessness and a sense of futility, lowered self-esteem, and a lack of responsibility for one's actions. Such children see little relationship between their actions and outcomes. They maintain what psychologists label an external locus of control. Events that happen to them are seen as externally directed. They take no ownership for such outcomes, either positive or negative. It is no small wonder that their behavior becomes rigidly stereotyped as aggressive and their relationships with others, destructive.

A residential treatment facility must provide a sense of safety and security. If the facility is not well structured and supervised, so that physical safety is in jeopardy, the child may as well be back on the streets from which he or she was allegedly rescued. If the child is still at risk from other children or, worse yet, from staff, no amount of therapy or caring will be effective. This assertion would seem to be unnecessary in a book devoted to child treatment. Yet, assaults within supposedly safe treatment settings are commonplace.

After safety, a residential facility must provide a sense of belonging. The children coalesce into a family. They often give each other designations of sister or brother. Until they become accepted by the group, new children are in jeopardy. They cannot function. As Polsky (1962) has noted, the peer subculture looms far more important than relationships with staff. However, once the child does bond with the group, he or she may then be free to relate to staff. The peer group gives permission, endorsing the relationships with staff. Sometimes a resident may challenge the staff member: "What you messing with him for? He's a faggot." Even the least accessible child may tentatively approach a staff member, seeking approval ("How come you ain't got no hair?"). Such overtures may signal that the child is ready to allow a closer relationship.

With a sense of belonging fostered by the treatment program, the child is in a position to reevaluate his or her own relationships with his or her family. The most dysfunctional families may still serve a purpose to the child in centering him- or herself somewhere in the universe. The relationship is reciprocal, and he or she may return psychologically to the family. This repositioning from the temporary and artificial family of the peer group subculture to the more permanent biological or foster family must take place eventually for successful family reunification.

The residential facility is in a position to help the child in the mastery of skills that are vital for living. With almost every child we have admitted, we have observed serious deficits in academic functioning. In many, these deficits are associated with learning disabilities. Cognitive deficits may result from neurological disorders such as fetal alcohol syndrome. They may also be associated with inadequate nutrition or poor prenatal care with children coming from backgrounds of poverty. Skills that require remediation include basic academics, social coping and community survival, and job training.

A high priority is placed on academics. The children referred for residential treatment typically have histories of failure and noncompliance in school settings. Many can barely read. Rather than expose their lack of competence, they will disrupt a classroom or fail to attend. Yet, they are aware of their shortcomings. They realize that they will need to have a job and that their poor skills will handicap them. They present educators with an almost insurmountable problem. Most important, the classroom must be made accessible to them. That means that academics should be made as nonthreatening as possible. Individual instruction must be provided to avoid forcing a child to expose his or her deficits. School must be made interesting, even fun. Learning must be concrete and practical. Yet, a therapeutic approach can be taken too far. These children are aware of what a normal school looks like. School cannot be a "cop-out" for them. They must perceive that real education is taking place, that school is not just used as a holding tank. One child demanded, "Where is the science and the social studies?" In a program that already provides many therapeutic modalities, more counseling in the classroom may be superfluous if it is substituted for old-fashioned academic basics.

Social skills and community functioning are equally important. The child needs as much supervised experience in the community as the facility can provide. Restaurants, parks, theaters, museums, YMCAs, public swimming pools, ballparks, concerts, and plays can all be used as training grounds. The appropriate use of leisure time activity is a skill that many children have never learned simply because they have not had the opportunity to be taken by parents to such events. Recently, I attended the Prokofiev ballet *Cinderella.* Because of the nature of the presentation, the audience consisted of a large number of children. Such events comprise a substantial part of the upbringing of middle- and upper-class children, so why not those with a child welfare background as well?

Autonomy is an important goal for any treatment program. We believe that autonomy includes two dimensions—internal locus of control and responsibility. The child must learn to recognize a connection between immediate behaviors and future outcomes. This is the potential of successful cognitive therapy as well as experiences of decision making and choice within the treatment program. Acceptance of an internal locus of control for positive and negative events produces a sense of power that can replace the chronic futility of children in placement. Furthermore, it can provide a sense of social responsibility. Once the child learns that he or she can determine his or her own fate, the next step is to recognize that he or she may have some influence over the lives of others.

The program provided by the residential treatment facility must go beyond the problem behaviors in addressing the unmet needs of the children as well as the underlying feelings and the most basic values. Behavior modification that addresses only the most visible behaviors will not offer a permanent solution. By manipulating outcomes (reinforcements), behavior modification may produce temporary improvements. The children may behave better within the treatment facility. However, unless their distorted view of the world as hostile and aggressive is changed, unless they learn to risk placing some trust in people, unless they are able to take ownership for their behavior and realize they have power to affect their own future, unless they accept societal standards of right and wrong, children will not be permanently affected by the residential experience.

Cornell physicist, Vinay Ambegaokar (1996), commenting on the creative process in the physical sciences, offered the consolation that, despite the challenges to researchers, "when the dust settles, it settles for good" (p. 2). Psychologists operate, unfortunately, in perpetually dusty environments with age-old conundrums about the nature of man continually reappearing in new guises. So, in the field of child welfare, research has not provided easy solutions to the most efficacious ways of healing battered children.

This book has reviewed a body of literature pertinent to the treatment of emotionally disturbed adolescents entering the child welfare system. As the reader has already discerned, there are no ready answers. Experts and advocates call for family preservation and family reunification as goals and for maximum opportunities for contact with the biological family when out-of-home placements are necessary. With the "least restrictive alternative" as a guiding principle, home-based services are seen as superior to out-of-home placements, foster care is judged more advantageous than congregate living situations, and group homes are more acceptable than large institutional settings. Yet, such choices are workable only on a macrolevel of programming. Within any treatment option, there must be a structured treatment approach implemented by caregivers, be they a foster family or a residential living specialist.

The most well-planned placement for a child can rapidly deteriorate into a situation far worse than that from which placement was made. Yet, many programs amount to little more than supervised living situations. If active treatment is applied, it may be without an overall treatment philosophy or plan. Counseling or psychotherapy for the child may be left solely to the discretion of the therapist, with no unifying connections to the residential phases of the placement. Program providers and implementers, hard pressed to meet regulatory requirements with the financial constraints imposed, often have little time to develop grand conceptual models for treatment. Yet, I argue here that attempts to provide remedial interventions with challenging children, no matter how well intended, may succeed only in providing a way station for the child in an endless succession of placements with negative outcomes. Similarly, the pressures of day-to-day program provision may leave little energy for assessment of program outcomes. Such has been the case in the child welfare system for well over the last century.

A traveler in a foreign country would secure a road map to navigate unfamiliar territory. In many ways, the children referred for residential treatment represent a largely uncharted terrain. If the analogy of a foreign country is too extreme, the reality of a different culture is difficult to dispute. CASSP principles embrace the need for cultural competence in treatment programs, but the intent there seems to relate to ethnic differences rather than the more subtle effects of poverty, family dysfunction or dissolution, and violence and abuse. Previous chapters have summarized some of the literature documenting the outcomes of these social problems and have attempted to relate their effects to traditional psychiatric nosological concepts. Unquestionably, more than traditional conceptualizations and approaches are demanded.

Just as the traveler abroad, planners and professionals require a road map to negotiate the vagaries of working with battered children. The problem cannot be resolved by any one worker, research center, or treatment facility. A national effort is called for, with a division of effort for developing and evaluating individual components of a broad-based treatment program. Are there effective interventions for social alienation, anger, despair, helplessness, and rebellion of children who have been poorly treated in families and schools and communities? Macrosolutions have no meaning without a detailed blueprint for change. Such a plan would need to identify the multifaceted components of personality disorganization or impairment that present themselves to child welfare workers and therapists dealing with battered children. Assessment procedures for defining the strengths and deficits need to be identified or developed, and finally, intervention approaches precisely spelled out. This chapter calls for such an approach and offers a humble beginning.

## *A TREATMENT MODEL*

Expanding from the model of Brendtro, Brokenleg, and Van Bockern (1990), a model for assessment and treatment is roughly outlined in this section. If the dimensions and skills suggested below are faulty, the model is correctable. I challenge workers in the field to coordinate their efforts toward an effective and unified treatment approach.

Drawing from traditional Native American child rearing philosophies, Brendtro and colleagues (1990) address the basic components of self-esteem by focusing upon four universal needs or values: belonging, mastery, independence, and generosity. A sense of belonging affords the individual significance in life by satisfying needs for attention, affection, attachment, and acceptance. Mastery brings a sense of competence within one's environment. Independence replaces helplessness with a sense of power. Generosity provides a feeling of worthiness and virtue. Healing children who are characterized by destructive relationships, futility, irresponsibility, and lack of purpose requires the provision of a nurturing environment that satisfies these four basic needs. Brendtro and colleagues list normal manifestations of the four needs as well-distorted attempts to gain satisfaction for these needs, e.g., promiscuous behavior to gain a sense of belonging.

General therapeutic approaches are discussed, such as the use of discipline versus punishment by teaching internalization of values rather than the arbitrary use of consequences. We endorse this approach but carry the process further by delineating areas of functioning that relate to five broad sectors of living (adding one dimension to Brendtro and colleagues) operating within four spheres of influence: self, family, school, and community.

While Brendtro and his colleagues see self-esteem as central to all four need systems, I find it reasonable to separate personal integrity as the most basic developmental milestone and a prerequisite for the other four needs. From birth, the infant learns a sense of identity that never ceases to be modified by experience. The earliest experience is the differentiation of self from nonself as the child senses his or her own body and its limits. Personal integrity encompasses self-esteem, self-control, self-concept, body image, and self-efficacy (later fading into mastery). A sense of safety and security within one's environment also adds to personal integrity. These components of the sense of self lead naturally to a sense of belonging in a nurturant family.

The model of Brendtro and his colleagues identifies "belonging" as a central need in children in placement and one that leads often to distorted expressions of this need. The likelihood that such children will manifest attachment disorders is high and consistent with inborn biological impairment, traumatic experiences in dysfunctional and sometimes abusive families, and multiple placements within the child welfare system. Associated with the attachment process are a range of prosocial values and behaviors including caring, friendliness, trust, gregariousness, cooperation, loyalty, and capacity for close interpersonal relationships. How are children, who have been unable to attach themselves to parents, siblings, and an extended family, to learn to form close relationships with others? Curiously, in the absence of early nurturance and the security inculcated in close, loving families, children do seek a sense of belonging within a peer culture, often embracing antisocial values. The challenge to foster parents and to residential treatment centers is to channel unmet needs for belonging into meaningful relationships with positive role models. As Polsky (1962) has pointed out, this may require interventions within the subcultural peer group, not apart from it.

Personality and social psychologists have repeatedly emphasized the relationship between self-esteem and the recognition of one's ability to be successful in valued activities (Bandura and Walters, 1959). The specific skills that make individuals feel good about themselves will differ. Emmitt Smith, Dallas Cowboys running back, probably feels no pangs about not writing scholarly papers in learned professional journals, and most people who do are long past caring about their ability to succeed as a pass receiver. Mastery of important skills is essential for healthy social development and a prerequisite for later independence. Children in placement have missed opportunities for normal social and academic learning associated with achievement, success, and competence in life. Revolving-door residential placements also mean revolving-door school placements with interruptions in the orderly instructional process. Remedial environments need to work from a detailed and specific skill development curriculum such as that developed by Bloomquist (1996).

Adolescence is a time of loosening of parental attachments and rebellion against family and societal values. When socialization has been impaired and parental attachments never firmly established, adolescent drives for autonomy occur without a framework of attenuating inhibitions. Hormonal surges and increasing physical prowess create an explosive internal state that may erupt in violence and antisocial behavior. A childhood of frustration and emotional deprivation finds its outlet in ways that incur the punitive arm of society. Recklessness and defiance become the acceptable norm, reinforced by deviant peer culture. Increasing independence, instead of fostering greater confidence and responsibility, exacerbates unbridled aggressive and destructive impulses.

The final dimension, labeled "generosity" by Brendtro and colleagues (1990) and termed "values" here, has been discussed in Chapter 9. Can we teach children to care about the welfare of others and to be sensitive to others' feelings much as if they were their own? Values clarification is in its infancy in intervention programs. There is little evidence that such attempts, even if widely implemented, would be effective. Yet, altruism and empathy would seem to be at the root of the inculcation of prosocial behavior. The opinion was offered that generalization from RTF experience to family and community settings requires cognitive changes, as described in both Chapters 8 and 9.

A first attempt to outline an assessment grid that can also serve as a curriculum development model is presented in the following paragraphs. No one facility or program would be sufficient to develop either the assessment component or the remedial program. The outline is offered tentatively here as the next step in expanding and implementing the model of Brendtro, Brokenleg, and Van Bockern (1990).

The model translates the four-needs system plus the general area of personal integrity into five sectors of living. Each of these sectors is expressed in a somewhat different fashion as the child enters four different spheres of functioning—self, family, school, and community. The intersection of each sector with each sphere suggests areas of competence that the child must accomplish during different developmental stages. This model should lead to meaningful differentiation and structuring of both evaluation and intervention efforts (see Figure 1).

Personal integrity refers to a sense of self or identity closely tied to self-esteem and self-efficacy. This sector encompasses the perception of being safe and secure in the environment. Finally, it includes a perception of being in control of one's body, impulses, and environment. In excess, a sense of personal integrity may signify self-centered egotism and the need to overcontrol others.

Belonging refers to the most basic mechanisms of attachment, developing from birth and leading to group identity required for prosocial, cooperative behaviors.

Mastery includes skill development and competencies in daily living, academic, social, and vocational areas.

Autonomy, building upon mastery skills, refers to independent functioning and self-reliance in all social settings and includes abilities in the areas of problem solving, decision making, judgment, and creativity.

Values refers to the development of a personal credo and a set of cognitions about the world that encompasses a sense of right and wrong, support for the rights of others, a capacity for empathy, and a respect for the personal integrity of other human beings.

When deficits or distortions exist in these sectors of living, they must be identified, and the child should be exposed to compensatory efforts of training.

The intersection of sectors of living and spheres of development results in a matrix of eighty-eight cells, numbered in Table 1. These

FIGURE 1. A Model for Training*

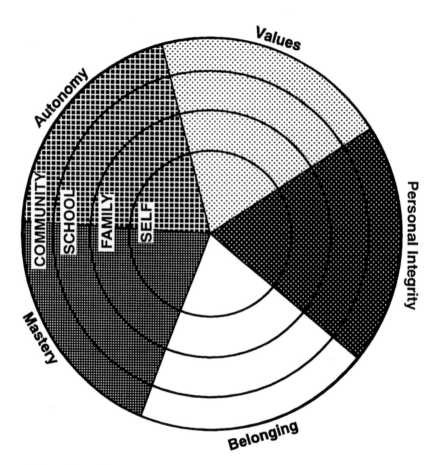

*Adapted from Brendtro, Brokenleg, and Van Bockern, 1990.

cells can form the basis of an intervention/evaluation grid. An attempt at an operational definition of the cells in this model is presented in the appendix.

The specter of managed care at this writing, early in 1997, will soon become a reality. Our county has already selected a managed

TABLE 1. Conceptual Model—88 Keys to Living
Intervention/Evaluation Grid

| Sector | Sphere | | | |
|---|---|---|---|---|
| | Self | Family | School | Community |
| **Personal Integrity** | | | | |
| Identity | 1Se | 1F | 1Sc | 1C |
| Self-control | 2Se | 2F | 2Sc | 2C |
| Self-esteem | 3Se | 3F | 3Sc | 3C |
| Self-efficacy | 4Se | 4F | 4Sc | 4C |
| Safety/security | 5Se | 5F | 5Sc | 5C |
| **Belonging** | | | | |
| Attachment | 6Se | 6F | 6Sc | 6C |
| Special relationship | 7Se | 7F | 7Sc | 7C |
| Cooperation | 8Se | 8F | 8Sc | 8C |
| **Mastery** | | | | |
| Activities of daily living | 9Se | 9F | 9Sc | 9C |
| Academic | 10Se | 10F | 10Sc | 10C |
| Social | 11Se | 11F | 11Sc | 11C |
| Vocational | 12Se | 12F | 12Sc | 12C |
| **Autonomy** | | | | |
| Independence | 13Se | 13F | 13Sc | 13C |
| Problem solving | 14Se | 14F | 14Sc | 14C |
| Decision making | 15Se | 15F | 15Sc | 15C |
| Judgment | 16Se | 16F | 16Sc | 16C |
| Creativity | 17Se | 17F | 17Sc | 17C |
| **Values** | | | | |
| Altruism | 18Se | 18F | 18Sc | 18C |
| Empathy | 19Se | 19F | 19Sc | 19C |
| Generosity | 20Se | 20F | 20Sc | 20C |
| Respect for others | 21Se | 21F | 21Sc | 21C |
| Right and wrong | 22Se | 22F | 22Sc | 22C |

care organization to administer medical assistance payments to county providers. Providers will be required to be part of a broad network of service options. Inpatient psychiatric services will be a necessity. No longer will we be able to select a psychiatric facility should a child require hospitalization. Rather, we will be obliged either to develop such a program ourselves or to affiliate with a program that we would use exclusively. Either option is not necessarily bad since it should allow a partnership arrangement with shorter stays for the child and a more facile flow of information between the two facilities. Cross relationships between the two staff complements would provide interesting opportunities for professional growth.

Another requirement will undoubtedly be a greater demand for credentialing of persons providing services. Over the past several decades, some erosion of professionalism has occurred in the provision of human services. The proliferation of community services has created more demand for psychologists, social workers, and therapists, but the equally rapid expansion of HMOs, PPOs, and other third-party providers has often allowed less well-trained professionals into the system. Empowerment of handicapped populations and the emphasis on the rights of such persons to enter the decision-making process, although having many positive repercussions, has also taken authority away from professionals. Some would argue that such is not the case, i.e., it is not a "zero sum game" with only a finite amount of power and control to go around. Yet, many decisions are now made on the basis of political demands, however defensible they may be, rather than on clinical rationale. Team decisions seem to have replaced the authoritative decisions of one or two professionals. Insistence upon accountability by credentialed professionals may reverse this process. A pressure is also being exerted to bring treatment programs for emotionally disturbed individuals more directly under medical control. In Pennsylvania, there are fiscal advantages for accreditation of RTFs under regulations of the Joint Commission on the Accreditation of Hospitals (JCAHO). According to such regulations, the clinical program must be under the direction of a psychiatrist. Managed care may insist upon JCAHO accreditation of providers. However, JCAHO programs are more expensive so that economics may militate against such accreditation.

The following imperatives are seen as critical to the RTF and are presently unaddressed:

1. Develop a state-of-the-art clinical treatment program, progressing from a largely regulation driven to a clinically driven approach.
2. Integrate medical, biological, psychiatric, and psychosocial components.

3. Integrate a sophisticated diagnostic assessment into the treatment process.
4. Establish viable exits from the program.
5. Maintain quality treatment in spite of rapid growth, new target populations, and new service needs.
6. Transform direct care staff into clinical agents of change.
7. Develop a philosophical/conceptual program focus.
8. Teach children enduring values, self-control, and motivation that will generalize to community and home living.
9. Improve program quality in the face of anticipated budgetary restraints with managed care.

With over a century of minimal success in learning to manage child welfare populations and thorny questions still unanswered, is there reason for optimism? The answer is a guarded affirmative. I find reason to be hopeful within the mental health disciplines themselves. I submit that a sufficient base about the etiology of emotional disturbance in children already exists, as does the technologies to treat such problems. What has been lacking is not information but the resolve to apply our knowledge and techniques in an aggressive and consistent manner.

Environmental variables undoubtedly contribute significantly to the problems faced by children being referred to residential treatment centers. Deprivation, neglect, and abuse are already correctly identified as determining factors. Faulty parenting, providing coercive and inconsistent methods of control, undoubtedly contributes. Inadequate learning of negotiating and problem-solving skills and the motivation to use them characterize most of the children we encounter in residential placement. There is nothing being reported in contemporary journals and textbooks that was not identified and appreciated generations ago in children presenting similar problems.

Furthermore, psychotherapy and counseling work. Intensive interventions which are performed within a carefully nurtured therapeutic relationship and which consistently utilize sound theoretical formulations work. Children do survive separations and loss of families. They survive foster placements, and they survive residential treatment facilities. Not all children growing up in poverty-stricken areas develop conduct disorders or become delinquents. A child may be helped to build self-esteem, and mechanisms exist for empowering a child to overcome feelings of helplessness and to become motivated to achieve.

Why, then, have we been so ineffective in applying these technologies? One answer lies in the volume of children who require help and the limited resources mental health professionals are able to martial for this purpose. The burden of day-to-day operations for large numbers of children grouped unnaturally into congregate living facilities is daunting. Professionals themselves become inured to the problems of the children and pessimistic about outcomes. Self-efficacy of staff working in such settings may become eroded. Staff burnout in such settings has been repeatedly reported. The relentless succession of challenges presented on a twenty-four hour, 365-day basis engenders pessimism and discouragement. We tend to blame ourselves for failures, which are many, and to overlook successes, which may be sparse. We doubt our own effectiveness. Most important, we neglect our own training to accurately and objectively evaluate what we are doing.

I end this book not by indicting the child welfare or mental health systems but by calling for a renewal of efforts to evaluate our past attempts in order to objectively understand what we have done right and where we could have done better. The number of children passing through RTFs must be monitored and their outcomes evaluated. We need to be honest in our criteria of success or failure and to assign the most honest outcome to each child possible. Did the year or two of residential treatment have any impact upon the child and his family? Once we have accomplished that task objectively, we can go back to files and to staff and attempt to determine what went wrong and what was judged to be beneficial. Correlational analyses may reveal what is not immediately obvious in identifying possible determining factors. Such studies should be performed routinely and without preconceived notions.

Clinicians repeatedly must renew themselves as treatment agents and rededicate themselves to whatever theoretical and treatment approaches make sense. Finally, they need to become more effective advocates for these children, refusing to accept the least common denominator of residential treatment and care, while working with administrators, business, and fiscal people to let them know exactly what is needed to create innovative and effective treatment.

# Epilogue

The two friends met regularly for dinner, but the topic did not arise again for over a year. Then, unexpectedly, the second received a large package from the author. The manuscript was over 250 typewritten pages.

"It's done," explained the brief note. "Let me know what you think."

Dutifully, the friend began reading. The discussion of the previous year came back to mind as well as the suggestion he had made.

Later, when they met, he asked why the author had not gone all the way and written a more readable book. Why had he maintained the academic style in most of the chapters?

"I didn't have the confidence that I could pull it off. I tried a more popular style many years ago, and although I was able to find a publisher, the book did not sell. It was an ego trip and little more. At first, I wanted to include case studies of the children, but it would violate their privacy, even if I changed their names. Informed consent was not possible in most cases. Confidentiality and liability issues surfaced. I stuck with review chapters of issues I felt to be relevant. RTFs are springing up all over the country. People should have some idea of what they are about—more than just idle chatter. Perhaps the book will provide an anchor."

\* \* \*

The writer gave the manuscript a last look before he mailed it off.
"Hey, white boy. You own this building?"
Inwardly, he knew his friend was right.

\* \* \*

This book underwent a major transformation midway through the writing. The original plan was to document the development of a residential treatment facility and to present the stories of many of the children involved. In addition, a number of review-style chapters would provide some theoretical and empirical underpinning for the treatment program. About a dozen of the children were profiled in case studies or through counseling sessions. This plan was changed when both ethical and legal considerations became apparent. The code of ethical principles endorsed by the American Psychological Association mandates that privacy of the persons depicted be preserved. Although it is typical that name changes and minor alteration of details are used to maintain anonymity, in this case, the events were sufficiently revealing to make it likely that the child could be identified by the family and the staff at the facility. The stories typically involved abuse and sometimes abandonment by the families. Furthermore, many of the families were not available to provide consent. The protective agencies that maintained custody would probably have decided in favor of not compromising the child's and family's privacy.

I obsessed over this issue for many weeks, conferring with colleagues, the agency's legal counsel, and the publisher. In the end, I decided to eliminate about one hundred pages of case history material.

The text that remains now consists solely of review chapters. I hope the book provides a fair depiction of the issues involved in placing children, while still retaining some popular appeal.

*Marvin Rosen*

# Appendix

## OPERATIONAL DEFINITIONS
## FOR CONCEPTUAL MODEL

### Personal Integrity

- 1Se (identity/self)
  Knowledge of own name, age, gender, RTF address
  Sense of ownership of possessions
  Awareness of own history; sense of continuity
  Awareness of certain attributes that are uniquely one's own

- 1F (identity/family) Note: This item assesses sense of awareness or belonging only as an association, not as a sense of positive attachment. It refers to inclusion only as being a member of a set, not as an affinity for members of that set.
  Sense of role within a family, e.g., second child of Mr. and Mrs. ____; sister of _____
  Awareness of more distant family relationships (uncles, aunts, cousins, grandparents)
  Location of a family unit geographically

- 1Sc (identity/school) See Note 1F
  Awareness of enrollment in a specific community-based school prior to RTF enrollment; identifies approximate location
  Awareness of grade-level placement at that school

- 1C (identity/community) See Note 1F
  Awareness of home address including city or town
  Conversant about certain characteristic features; e.g., shopping centers, parks, recreational areas

- 2Se (self-control/self) Note: This item refers solely to a sub-jective sense of control, regardless of whether the child is hyperactive or impulsive.

  Sense of control over own body; feeling that motor behavior, actions, and emotions are under control

  The opposite would be a sense of helplessness in controlling behavior and emotions.

- 2F (self-control/family)

  Sense of being in control of relationship within a family

  The family structure is perceived as stable as is the child's own perceived role in that family, e.g., "I am the child in a specific family and this will not change."

- 2Sc (self-control/school)

  Sense of control in being able to function in school

- 2C (self-control/community)

  Sense of control in being able to function in a larger geo-graphic unit (neighborhood, community) and being relatively stable in that community

- 3Se (self-esteem/self)

  Generally positive evaluation of one's own attributes

  Sense of enduring nature of certain positive attributes

  Attributes may be physical features, abilities, achievements, or skills.

- 3F (self-esteem/family) Note: This area is scored positive only if the child shares in the positive attributes by virtue of his or her membership in the family.

  Generally positive evaluation of the child's own family unit

  This is evidenced by positive references of family or its attrib-utes, e.g., "My father has a good job" or "My brothers always do well in school."

- 3Sc (self-esteem/school) Note: This area is scored positive only if the child shares in the positive attribute by virtue of being a student at that school.

  Generally positive evaluation of the community school with which the child identifies, e.g., "My school always has a great football team."

- 3C (self-esteem/community) Note: This area is scored positive only if the child shares in the attribute by virtue of being a resident of that community.

  Generally positive evaluation of home neighborhood or community with which the child identifies, e.g., "Springfield has great parks."

- 4Se (self-efficacy/self)

  Child expresses a sense of mastery of certain skills that he or she judges as critical to self-esteem, e.g., "I am good at videogames" or "I am a good pitcher."

- 4F (self-efficacy/family)

  Child believes he or she can meet family expectations at home.

- 4Sc (self-efficacy/school)

  Same as 4Se but skills are specifically related to academic functioning or to social functioning at school, e.g., "I am good at reading."

- 4C (self-efficacy/community)

  Same as 4Se but skills are specifically related to a community or neighborhood group or activity, e.g., "I made Eagle Scout."

- 5Se (safety/security/self)

  Child expresses a sense of safety about his or her person. He or she feels relatively free from physical danger, illness, and assault.

- 5F (safety/security/family)

  Same as 5Se, specifically in family

- 5Sc (safety/security/school)

  Sane as 5Se, specifically in school

- 5C (safety/security/community)

  Same as 5Se, specifically in home community or neighborhood

## Belonging

- 6Se (Attachment/self)

  This is a nonrated cell.

- 6F (attachment/family)

  Child expresses a feeling of belonging to a family. He or she takes ownership of that family and expresses positive feelings of attachment/closeness to one or more members of his or her primary or foster family. This cell measures more than merely identification as a member of a family by birth or circumstance. It must involve some emotional component of a positive nature.

- 6Sc (attachment/school)

  Positive feeling and closeness to friends or teachers at his or her home school

- 6C (attachment/community)

  Positive feeling to friends or neighbors in the child's immediate neighborhood

- 7Se (special relationship/self)

  This is a nonrated cell.

- 7F (special relationship/family)

  This is a more intense feeling toward some family member involving a special closeness or relationship.

  It requires a positive rating on 6F as prerequisite.

- 7Sc (special relationship/school)

  This is a more intense feeling toward a person at school who could be a special buddy or confidant, including a teacher.

  It requires a positive rating on 6Sc as prerequisite.

- 7C (special relationship/community)

  This is a more intense rating toward a friend in the neighborhood or community.

  It requires a positive rating on 6C as prerequisite.

- 8Se (cooperation/self)

  This is a nonrated cell.

- 8F (cooperation/family)

  A cooperative relationship between the child and one or more persons in the family in working toward some common goal

  It does not require a special emotional bond.

- 8Sc (cooperation/school)

  A cooperative relationship with a child or teacher at school in working toward a common goal

  It does not require a special emotional bond.

- 8C (cooperation/community)

  A cooperative relationship with a friend or neighbor in the community

  It does not require a special emotional bond.

## *Mastery*

(These ratings reflect actual skill levels rather than subjective feelings of the child.)

- 9Se (ADL/self)

  Mastery of self-help skills appropriate for an adolescent including personal hygiene, dressing, and eating

- 9F (ADL/family)

  Mastery of skills required for family living including basic house-keeping, cooking, and chores appropriate for an adolescent

- 9Sc (ADL/school)

  Mastery of basic behaviors required to attend school including getting up on time, using the school bus, attending to material, maintaining responsibility for books, obeying school rules for discipline, and attendance

- 9C (ADL/community)

  Mastery of basic community skills such as ability to move freely in the neighborhood, use public transportation, cross streets safely, use the telephone, go shopping, and manage money

- 10Se (academic/self)

  This is a nonrated cell.

- 10F (academic/family)

  Ability to complete homework assignments independently or with a minimal degree of supervision

- 10Sc (academic/school)

  Ability to function satisfactorily at grade level and progress academically at a regular pace

- 10C (academic/community)

  Ability to use community resources as needed to satisfy academic requirements (e.g., use a library)

- 11Se (social/self)

  Mastery of sufficient social skills to establish and maintain interpersonal relationships including skills related to sports and recreational activities and being acceptable to peers

- 11F (social/family)

  Mastery of necessary social skills for harmonious relationships within a family setting

  Ability to perform role as child, sibling

  Ability to integrate within a family setting with excessive disruptive behavior

- 11Sc (social/school)
  Mastery of necessary social skills for harmonious relationships within a school setting
  Ability to perform role of student, classmate

- 11C (social/community)
  Mastery of social skills for socialization within neighborhood or community including staying out of trouble, avoiding legal difficulties, and being a good citizen

- 12Se (vocational/self)
  This is a nonrated cell.

- 12F (vocational/family)
  This is a nonrated cell.

- 12Sc (vocational/school)
  This area is rated if the child is in a vocational program at school and has mastered a vocational or prevocational skill appropriate to his or her age and the program.

- 12C (vocational/community)
  Mastery of sufficient vocational skills to maintain a community job on at least a part-time basis
  The child must currently have such a job to receive a rating here.

### Autonomy

(These ratings will require high levels of skill mastery as prerequisites.)

- 13Se (independence/self)
  Demonstrated competence in assuming responsibility for oneself without monitoring or supervision
  The individual can be left alone with instructions to maintain self-control, complete tasks or chores, handle routine situations that may arise, and take messages.

- 13F (independence/family)
  Same as 13Se but specifically in a family setting
  This may involve baby-sitting for a younger sibling, house-sitting, caring for pets, running errands, maintaining cleanliness of own room, and preparing meals.

- 13Sc (independence/school)
  Demonstrated competence in self-direction in negotiating requirements in a normal secondary school including being able to be mobile (as allowed) in finding classrooms and offices, following class schedules, and completing assignments

- 13C (independence/community)
  Demonstrated capability to move freely in the community, be responsible for time schedules and commitments, assume responsibilities within the community (e.g., delivering newspapers; shoveling snow for a neighbor; baby-sitting for a neighbor), and arrange for these responsibilities independently

- 14Se (problem solving/self)
  Demonstrated competence in independent problem solving including resolving minor conflicts or disagreements with friends, negotiating compromises, persuading others, enlisting help, showing initiative, using trial and error approaches, and showing perseverance after initial failure

- 14F (problem solving/family)
  Same as 14Se but specific to family situations

- 14Sc (problem solving/school)
  Same as 14Se but specific to school or academic situations

- 14C (problem solving/community)
  Same as 14Se but specific to community or neighborhood situations

- 15Se (decision making/self)
  Ability to make decisions concerning life events including identification and weighting of contributing factors
  Rated conservatively as a high-level cognitive skill

- 15F (decision making/family)
Same as 15Se but specific to family living situations
This may include input in placement decisions for children in out-of-home placements.

- 15Sc (decision making/school)
Same as 15Se but specific to school/career situations
This may include selection of program, track, or course concentration (e.g., enrollment in vocational school).

- 15C (decision making/community)
Same as 15Se but specific to community
This may include decisions about joining teams, clubs, or recreational programs, especially those requiring some degree of commitment and follow-through.

- 16Se (judgment/self)
Demonstration of mature judgment regarding decisions and behavior
This is a qualitative rating based upon what would be expected of normal adolescents. Judgment requires a recognition of consequences and impact of one's behavior upon oneself and others.

- 16F (judgment/family)
Same as 16Se but specific to family situations
Examples of poor judgment might include decisions to remain out later than agreed upon time limits or breaking family rules.

- 16Sc (judgment/school)
Same as 16Se but specific to school or academics
Examples of poor judgment might include cutting classes or unexcused absences from school or failure to complete assignments.

- 16C (judgment/community)
Same as 16Se but specific to community situations
Poor judgment might include placing oneself in dangerous situations.

- 17Se (creativity/self)

  Demonstrated originality and initiative in independent action

  Rated conservatively

  Example might be use of the computer in handling a problem situation in a novel manner.

- 17F (creativity/family)

  Same as Se but specific to family situations

  Example might be calling 911 in an emergency.

- 17Sc (creativity/school)

  Same as 17Se but specific to school or academic situations

  Example might be a creative handling of a project or assignment.

- 17C (creativity/community)

  Same as 17Se but in community situations

## Values

- 18Se (altruism/self)

  Demonstrated evidence of willingness to help others when there is no apparent reward or benefit to the child

  The help afforded others must be of significant effort, risk, or cost to the individual.

- 18F (altruism/family)

  This cell is not rated.

- 18Sc (altruism/school)

  Same as 18Se but in a school setting

  An example would be helping a friend with homework on a voluntary basis.

- 18C (altruism/community)

  Same as 18Se but in the community

  An example would be volunteering to help collect food for needy people or donating own money earned for this purpose.

- 19Se (empathy/self)
General quality of being able to feel for others or to share their feelings

- 19F (empathy/family)
Demonstrated ability to place oneself into a family member's shoes, i.e., to view the world as that person does
Shows feeling for the emotions of another, especially for that person's negative feelings

- 19Sc (empathy/school)
Same as 19F but specific to people at school

- 19C (empathy/community)
Same as 19F but specific to a neighbor or community member

- 20Se (generosity/self)
General quality of being willing to give or share one's possessions or time without prospect of personal gain

- 20F (generosity/family)
Demonstrated willingness to share personal possessions or time with family members

- 20Sc (generosity/school)
Same as 20F but specific to schoolmates

- 20C (generosity/community)
Same as 20F but specific to friend or acquaintance in neighborhood or community

- 21Se (respect for others/self)
General quality of acceptance, tolerance, and respect for other people including their personal space, possessions, rights, identity, and personal integrity
Unwillingness to violate the boundaries of others without clear permission

- 21F (respect for others/family)

  Same as 21Se but specific to family members

- 21Sc (respect for others/school)

  Same as 21Se but specific to persons in school setting

- 21C (respect for others/community)

  Same as 21Se but specific to other people in the neighborhood or community

- 22Se (Right and wrong/self)

  Clear sense of a concept of right and wrong for either religious, moral, ethical, or philosophical reasons

  Ability to make decisions on basis of abstract principle of right and wrong, regardless of consequences

- 22F (right and wrong/family)

  Same as 22Se but specific to family situations, e.g., "It's not right to steal from my sister."

- 22Sc (right and wrong/school)

  Same as 22Se but specific to school settings, e.g., "It's wrong to cheat on a test."

- 22C (right and wrong/community)

  Same as 22Se but in community settings, e.g., "I wait for the green light to cross because it's the right thing to do."

## SPHERES OF LIVING ASSESSMENT FORM*

| Sector | Sphere | | | |
|---|---|---|---|---|
| | Self | Family | School | Community |
| **Personal Integrity** | | | | |
| Identity (1) | | | | |
| Self-control (2) | | | | |
| Self-esteem (3) | | | | |
| Self-efficacy (4) | | | | |
| Safety/security (5) | | | | |
| **Belonging** | | | | |
| Attachment (6) | | | | |
| Special relationship (7) | | | | |
| Cooperation (8) | | | | |
| **Mastery** | | | | |
| ADL (9) | | | | |
| Academic (10) | | | | |
| Social (11) | | | | |
| Vocational (12) | | | | |
| **Autonomy** | | | | |
| Independence (13) | | | | |
| Problem solving (14) | | | | |
| Decision making (15) | | | | |
| Judgment (16) | | | | |
| Creativity (17) | | | | |
| **Values** | | | | |
| Altruism (18) | | | | |
| Empathy (19) | | | | |
| Generosity (20) | | | | |
| Respect for others (21) | | | | |
| Right and wrong (22) | | | | |

*Score each cell + or −.

# Bibliography

Abel, E. L. (1984). *Fetal Alcohol Syndrome and Fetal Alcohol Effects*. New York: Plenum Press.

Achenbach, T. M. (1991a). *Manual for the Child Behavior Checklist and 1991 Profile*. Burlington, VT: University of Vermont.

Achenbach, T. M. (1991b). *Manual for the Youth Self-Report and 1991 Profile*. Burlington, VT: University of Vermont.

Addams, J. (1916). *Democracy and Social Ethics*. New York: Macmillan.

Adoption Assistance and Child Welfare Act of 1980. Public Law 96-272, 42 U.S.C. 671 (1980).

Allen, J. P. and Pfeiffer, S. I. (1991). Residential treatment of adolescents who do not return to their families. *Comprehensive Mental Health Care, 1,* 209-222.

Allport, G. (1961). *Pattern and Growth in Personality*. New York: Holt, Rinehart, and Winston.

Ambegaokar, V. (1996). A physicist's reflections, reminiscences, and ramblings on the theme: Memory and creativity. *Arts and Science Newsletter, 18,* 1, 2-3.

American Psychiatric Association. (1994). *Diagnostic and Statistical Manual of Mental Disorders,* Fourth Edition. Washington, DC: American Psychiatric Association.

Armsden, G. C. and Greenberg, M. T. (1987). The inventory of parent and peer attachment: Individual differences and their relationship to psychological well-being in adolescents. *Journal of Youth and Adolescence, 16,* 427-451.

Ayasse, R. H. (1995). Addressing the needs of foster children: The foster youth services program. *Social Work Education, 17,* 207-216.

Azar, B. (1995). Foster children get a taste of stability. *APA Monitor, 26,* 8-9.

Bagley, C. and King, K. (1990). *Child Sexual Abuse: The Search for Healing.* New York: Tavistock/Routledge.

Baker, B. L., Blacher, J., and Pfeiffer, S. L. (1993). Family involvement in residential treatment of children with psychiatric disorder and mental retardation. *Hospital and Community Psychiatry, 44,* 561-566.

Baker, B. L., Heller, T. L., Blacher, J., and Pfeiffer, S. I. (1995). Staff attitudes toward family involvement in residential treatment centers for children. *Psychiatric Services, 46,* 60-65.

Baker, D. (1972). Chromosome errors and antisocial behavior. *CRC Critical Reviews in Clinical Laboratory Sciences, 3,* 41-101.

Baker, D. B. (1988). The psychology of Leightner Witmer. *Professional School Psychology, 3,* 109-121.

Bandura, A. (1964). Identification of the learning of attitude. In E.B. Page (Ed.), *Readings for Educational Psychology.* New York: Harcourt, Brace, and World, pp. 261-288.

Bandura, A. and Walters, R. H. (1959). *Adolescent Aggression.* New York: Ronald Press.

Barden, J. (1991, January 6). After release from foster care, many turn to life on the streets. *The New York Times,* p. E-5.

Barker, P. (Ed.), (1974). *The Residential Psychiatric Treatment of Children.* London: Crosby, Lockwood, Staples.

Barr, M. (1904). *Mental Defectives: Their History, Treatment and Training.* Philadelphia: P. Blakisten's Sons.

Barr, M. (1908). The relation between tuberculosis and mental defect. Paper presented at the International Congress on Tuberculosis, Washington, DC: September 29, 1908.

Barr, M. (1909). The criminal irresponsible. *Alienist and Neurologist, 30,* 1-9.

Barr, M. (1911). The career of a moral imbecile. *Alienist and Neurologist, 32,* 1-19.

Barr, M. (1912). A trio of moral imbeciles. *The Medical Times,* July, 1-11.

Barr, M. (1914). Rescue: The story of Alburtus. *Alienist and Neurologist, 35,* 3-10.

Barth, R. P. (1993). Protecting the future of children and families from Pelton's dangerous reforms. *Social Work, 38,* 98-100.

Batson, C. D. (1987). Prosocial motivation: Is it ever really altruistic? In L. Berkopwitz (Ed.), *Advances in Experimental Social Psychology.* Volume 20. New York: Academic Press, pp. 65-122.

Batson, C. D., Batson, J. G., Griffitt, C. A., Barrientos, S., Brandt, J. R., Sprengelmeyer, P., and Bayly, M. J. (1989). Negative-state relief and the empathy-altruism hypothesis. *Journal of Personality and Social Psychology, 56,* 922-933.

Beck, A. T., Rush, A. J., Shaw, B. F., and Emery, G. (1979). *Cognitive Therapy of Depression: A Treatment Manual.* New York: Guilford Press.

Begab, M. J., Haywood, H. C., and Garber, H. L. (Eds.), (1981). *Psychosocial Factors in Human Performance.* Volumes 1 and 2. Baltimore: University Park Press.

Bell, C. C. and Jenkins, E. J. (1991). Traumatic stress and children. *Journal of Health Care for the Poor and Underserved, 2,* 175-185.

Berkowitz, L. (1962). *Aggression: A Social Psychological Analysis.* New York: McGraw-Hill.

Bloomquist, M. L. (1996). *Skills Training for Children With Behavior Disorders: A Parent and Therapist Guidebook.* New York: The Guilford Press.

Boswell, J. (1988). *The Kindness of Strangers.* New York: Pantheon Books.

Bowlby, J. (1969). *Attachment and Loss.* Volume 1, *Attachment.* New York: Basic Books.

Bowlby, J. (1973). *Attachment and Loss.* Volume 2, *Separation.* New York: Basic Books.

Bowlby, J. (1980). *Attachment and Loss.* Volume 3, *Loss.* New York: Basic Books.

Bradley, M. and Aldgate, J. (1994). Sort-term family based care for children in need. *Adoption and Fostering, 18,* 24-28.

Brendtro, L. K. (1980). Bridging teaching and treatment: The American educateur. *Journal of Teacher Education, 21,* 23-26.

Brendtro, L. K. and Ness, A. E. (1996). Fixing flaws or building strengths. *Journal of Emotional and Behavioral Problems, 4,* 2-7.

Brendtro, L. K., Brokenleg, M., and Van Bockern, S. (1990). *Reclaiming Youth at Risk: Our Hope for the Future.* Bloomington, IN: National Educational Service.

Call, K. T., Mortimer, J. L., and Shanahan, M. J. (1995). Helpfulness and the development of competence in adolescence. *Child Development, 66,* 129-138.

Cianaldi, R. B., Schaller, M., Houlihan, D., Arps, K., Fultz, J., and Beaman, A. L. (1987). Empathy-based helping: Is it selflessly or selfishly motivated? *Journal of Personality and Social Psychology, 52,* 749-758.

Cimons, M. (1989, December 12). Minors in foster care put at 500,000. *Los Angelos Times,* p. A-4.

Clark, H. B., Prange, M. E., Lee, B. L., Boyd, A., McDonald, B. A., and Stewart, E. S. (1994). Improving adjustment outcomes for foster children with emotional and behavioral disorders: Early findings from a controlled study on individualized services. *Journal of Emotional and Behavioral Disorders, 2,* 207-218.

Cleckley, H. (1964). *The Mask of Sanity.* Fourth edition. St. Louis, MO: Kosby.

Cleland, C. C. and Peck, R. F. (1967). Intra-institutional administrative problems: A paradigm for employee stimulation. *Mental Retardation, 5,* 2-8.

Coles, R. (1997). *The Moral Intelligence of Children.* New York: Random House.

Connors, C. K. (1997). *Conners' Rating Scales-Revised.* North Tonawanda, NY: Multi-Health Systems.

Court Brown, W. M. (1968). Males with an XYY chromosome complement. *Journal of Medical Genetics, 5,* 341-343.

Courtois, C. (1979). The incest experience and its aftermath. *Victimology: An International Journal, 4,* 337-347.

Cravens, H. (1993). Child saving in modern America 1870s-1990s. In R. Wollons (Ed.), *Children at Risk in America: History, Concepts, and Public Policy.* Albany: State University of New York Press, pp. 3-31.

Crissey, M. S. (1975). Mental retardation: Past, present and future. *American Psychologist, 30,* 800-808.

Crissey, M. S. and Rosen, M. (Eds.), (1986). *Institutions for the Mentally Retarded.* Austin, TX: Pro-Ed.

Crowe, R. (1974). An adoption study of the antisocial personality. *Archives of General Psychiatry, 31,* 785-791.

Culliman, D., Gadow, K. D., and Epstein, M. H. (1987). Psychotropic drug treatment among learning disabled, educable mentally retarded, and seriously emotionally disturbed students. *Journal of Abnormal Child Psychology, 15,* 469-477.

Curwin, R. L. (1993). The healing power of altruism. *Educational Leadership, 51,* 3, November, 36-39.

Daly, P. M. (1985). The educateur: An atypical childcare worker. *Behavioral Disorders, 11,* 35-41.

Deblinger, E., McLeer, S. V., and Henry, D. (1989). Cognitive behavioral treatment for sexually abused children suffering post-traumatic stress: Preliminary findings. *Journal of the American Academy of Child and Adolescent Psychiatry, 29,* 747-752.

Dillon, D. (1994). Understanding and assessment of intragroup dynamics in family foster care: African American families. *Child Welfare, 73,* 129-139.

Dingman, H. F. and Tarjan, G. (1960). Mental retardation and the normal distribution curve. *American Journal of Mental Deficiency, 64,* 991-994.

Dollard, J., Doob, L., Miller, N., Mowrer, O. H., and Sears, R. (1939). *Frustration and Aggression.* New Haven: Yale University Press.

Drell, M., Siegel, C., and Gaensbauer, T. (1993). Post-traumatic stress disorders. In C. H. Zeanah (Ed.), *Handbook of Infant Mental Health.* New York: Guilford Press, pp. 291-304.

Dugdale, R. L. (1875). Hereditary pauperism as illustrated in the "Jukes" family. In I.C. Barrows (Ed.), *Proceedings of the Conference of Charities.* American Social Science Association. Detroit, May, 1875. Boston: Tolman and White, 81-96.

Dugdale, R. L. (1877) *The Jukes: A Study in Crime, Pauperism, Disease, and Heredity.* New York: Putnam.

Ellis, A. (1974). Rational emotive therapy. In A. Burson (Ed.), *Operational Theories of Personality.* New York: Brunner/Mazel, pp. 308-344.

Epstein, M. H. (1996). Serving children with serious emotional disturbance: The need to get real in the decade ahead. Paper presented at the Sixth Annual Virginia Beach Conference, Children and Adolescents with Emotional and Behavioral Disorders. Richmond, VA: October 4-8, 1996.

Exner, J. E. (1986). *The Rorschach: A Comprehensive System. Basic Foundation.* Volume 1. New York: Wiley.

Exner, J. E. and Weiner, I. B. (1982). *The Rorschach: A Comprehensive System. Assessment of Children and Adolescents.* New York: Wiley.

Fernald, W. E. (1893). The history of the treatment of the feeble-minded. *Proceedings of the Twentieth National Conference of Charities and Correction.* Boston: Ellis, p. 321.

Fernald, W. E. (1924). Thirty years progress in the care of the feeble-minded. *Journal of Psycho-Asthenics, 29,* 206-219.

Fraser, M. W. (1996). Aggressive behavior in childhood and early adolescence: An ecological-developmental perspective on youth violence. *Social Work, 41,* 347-361.

Friedrich, W. N. (1995). *Psychotherapy with Sexually Abused Boys: An Integrated Approach.* Thousand Oaks, CA: Sage Publications.

Friedrich, W. N., Luecke, W. J., Bielke, R. L., and Place, V. (1992). Psychotherapy outcome of sexually abused boys: An agency study. *Journal of Interpersonal Violence, 7,* 396-409.

Gadow, K. D. (1986). *Children on Medication: Epilepsy, Emotional Disturbance, and Adolescent Disorders*. Boston: College-Hill.

Galaway, B., Nutter, R. W., and Hudson, J. (1995). Relationship between discharge outcomes for treatment foster-care clients and program characteristics. *Journal of Emotional and Behavioral Disorders, 3*, 46-54.

Galdston, R. (1965). Observation in children who have been physically abused and their parents. *American Journal of Psychiatry, 122*, 440-443.

Gall, F. J. (1835). *On the Organ of the Moral Qualities and Intellectual Faculties and the Plurality of the Cerebral Organs*. Trans. W. Lewis. Boston, MA: Marsh, Coper, and Lyon.

Garber, H. L. (1988). *The Milwaukee Project: Preventing Mental Retardation in Children at Risk*. Washington, DC: American Association on Mental Retardation.

Gardner, J. M. (1968). Leightner Witmer—A neglected pioneer. *American Journal of Mental Deficiency, 72*, 719-720.

Geer, J. H. and Jermecky, L. (1973). The effect of being responsible for reducing another's pain on subjects' response and arousal. *Journal of Personality and Social Psychology, 26*, 232-237.

Gelinas, D. J. (1983). The persistent negative effects of incest. *Psychiatry, 46*, 312-332.

Gil, E. (1991). *The Healing Power of Play: Therapy with Abused Children*. New York: Guilford Press.

Gil, E. (1996). *Treating Abused Adolescents*. New York: Guilford Press.

Gil, E. and Johnson, T. C. (1993). *Sexualized Children: Evaluation and Treatment of Sexualized Children and Children Who Molest*. Rockville, MD: Launch Press.

Gleeson, J. P. (1995). Kinship care and public child welfare: Challenges and opportunities for social work education. *Journal of Social Work Education, 31*, 182-193.

Goddard, H. (1912). *The Kallikak family: A Study in the Heredity of Feeblemindedness*. New York: Macmillan.

Goerge, R. M., Van Voorhis, J., Grant, S., Casey, K., and Robinson, M. (1992). Special education experiences of foster children: An empirical study. *Child Welfare, 71*, 419-437.

Goodman, S. H. and Brumley, H. E. (1990). Schizophrenic and depressed mothers: Relational deficits in parenting. *Developmental Psychology, 26*, 31-39.

Green, A. H. (1978). Psychopathology of abused children. *Journal of Child Psychiatry, 17*, 92-103.

Greenhill, L. L. and Setterberg, S. (1993). Pharmacotherapy of disorders of adolescence. *Psychiatric Clinics of North America, 16*, 793-815.

Gregg, V., Gibbs, J. C., and Basinger, K. S. (1994). Patterns of developmental delay in moral judgment by male and female delinquents. *Merrill-Palmer Quarterly, 40*, 538-553.

Gries, L. T. (1986) The use of multiple goals in the treatment of foster children with emotional disorders. *Professional Psychology: Research and Practice, 17*, 381-390.

Hagan, F. E. (1994). *Introduction to Criminology: Theories, Methods, and Criminal Behavior.* Chicago, IL: Nelson-Hall.

Hartshorn, H. and May, M. A. (1928; 1929). *Studies in the Nature of Character.* Volume 1, *Studies in Deceit.* Volume 2, *Studies in Self-Control.* New York: Macmillan.

Hasci, T. (1995). From indenture to family foster care: A brief history of child placing. *Child Welfare, 74,* 162-180.

Heibert-Murphy, D., deLuca, R. V., and Runtz, M. (1992). Group treatment for sexually abused girls: Evaluating outcome. *Families in Society, 73,* 205-213.

Herman, J. L. (1981). *Father-Daughter Incest.* Cambridge, MA: Harvard University Press.

Hobbs, N. (1982). *The Troubled and Troubling Child.* San Francisco: Jossey-Bass.

Hobbs, N. (1983). Project Re-ED: From demonstration project to nationwide program. *Peabody Journal of Education, 60,* 8-24.

Hodapp, R. M. and Dykens, E. M. (1994). Mental retardation's two cultures of behavioral research. *American Journal on Mental Retardation, 98,* 675-687.

Hoffman, M. L. (1975). Developmental synthesis of affect and cognition and its implications for altruistic motivation. *Developmental Psychology, 11,* 607-622.

Hogan, R. (1993). Can deviants be morally educated? *The Social Studies, 84,* 271-275.

Howe, S. G. (1848). Report of commission to inquire into the conditions of idiots of the Commonwealth of Massachusetts. Boston, MA: Senate Document, No. 51, pp. 1-37.

Hunt, J. McV. (1961). *Intelligence and Experience.* New York: Ronald Press.

Hutchings, B. and Mednick, S. A. (1977). Criminality in adoptees and their adoptive and biological parents: A pilot study. In S. A. Mednick and K. O. Christensen (Eds.), *Biosocial Bases of Criminal Behavior.* New York: Gardner Press, pp. 127-142.

Itard, J. M. G. (1806). *Rapports et Memoirs sur de sauvage de l'Aveyron.* Trans. G. Humphrey. Reprinted (1930). New York: The Century Company.

Jacobs, P. A., Price, W. H., Brown, W. H., Brittain, R. P., and Whatmore, P. B. (1968). Chromosome studies on men in a maximum security hospital. *Annals of Human Genetics, 31,* 339-347.

Jendryka, B. (1991). Flanagan's island: How Boys Town rescues troubled teens. *Policy Review, 69,* 44-51.

Karp, R. J., Qazi, Q. H., Moller, K. A., Angelo, W. A., and Davis, J. M. (1995). Fetal alcohol syndrome at the turn of the 20th century: An unexpected explanation of the Kallikak family. *Archives of Pediatric Adolescent Medicine, 149,* 45-48.

Kazdin, A. E. (1988). *Child Psychotherapy.* Boston: Allyn and Bacon.

Kazdin, A. E. (1990). Conduct disorder in childhood. In M. Hersen and C. C. Last, *Handbook of Child and Adult Psychopathology: A Longitudinal Perspective.* New York: Pergamon Press.

Kendall-Tackett, K. A., Williams, L. M., and Finkelhor, D. (1993). The impact of sexual abuse on children: A review and synthesis of recent empirical studies. *Psychological Bulletin, 113,* 1, 164-180.

Kerlin, I. N. (1880). Enumeration, classification and causation of idiocy. *Transactions of the Medical Society of the State of Pennsylvania for 1980.* Philadelphia: Collins, p. 8.

Kerlin, I. N. (1889). Moral imbecility. *Proceedings of the Association of Medical Officers of American Institutions for Idiotic and Feeble-Minded Persons.* Lakeville, NJ: pp. 32-37.

Kerlin, I. N. (1976). Moral imbecility. In M. Rosen, G. R. Clark, and M. S. Kivitz (Eds.), *The History of Mental Retardation: Collected Papers,* Volume 1. Baltimore, MD: University Park Press, pp. 303-310. (Original work published 1889.)

Kessler, S. and Moos, R. H. (1969). XYY chromosomes: Premature conclusions. *Science, 165,* 442-444.

King, R. (1991). Emergence of self-destructive phenomena in children and adolescents during Fluoxetine treatment. *Journal of the American Academy of Child and Adolescent Psychiatry, 179.*

Kohlberg, L. (1969). Stage and sequence: The cognitive-developmental approach to socialization. In D. Goslin (Ed.), *Handbook of Socialization Theory and Research.* New York: Rand McNally, pp. 347-480.

Krug, S. (1983). *Interpreting 16PF Profile Patterns.* Champaign, IL: Institute for Personality and Ability Testing.

Kutash, K. (1995). Effectiveness of children's mental health services: A review of the literature. *Education and Treatment of Children, 18,* 443-477.

Lakin, K. C., Bruininks, R. H., Hill, B. K., and Hauber, F. A. (1982). Turnover of direct-care staff in a national sample of residential facilities for mentally retarded people. *American Journal of Mental Deficiency, 87,* 64-72.

Lanktree, C. B. and Briere, J. (1995). Outcome of therapy for sexually abused children: A repeated measures study. *Child abuse and neglect, 19,* 1145-1155.

Laufer, Z. (1990). Family ties as viewed by child care and treatment personnel in residential settings for children aged 5-14. *Child and Youth Care Quarterly, 19,* 49-57.

Lazarus, A. A. (1976). *Multimodal Behavior Therapy.* New York: Springer.

Locke, J. (1804). *Essay Concerning Human Understanding.* E. Campbell (Ed.), New York: Fraser. (See also: *The Clarendon Edition of the Works of John Locke.* [1975]. Oxford: Clarendon Press.)

Loftus, E. F. (1993). The reality of repressed memories. *American Psychologist, 48,* 518-537.

Lombrosso, C. (1973). Introduction. In A. MacDonald, *Criminology* (Reprint Edition). New York: AMS Press (original work published in 1893).

Loranger, A. W., Oldham, J. M., and Tulis, E. H. (1982). Familial transmission of DSM-III borderline personality disorder. *Archives of General Psychiatry, 39,* 795-799.

Lyman, S. B. and Bird, G. W. (1996). A closer look at self-image in male foster care adolescents. *Social Work, 41,* 85-96.

Manderscheid, R. W. and Sonnenschein, M. A. (1992). *Mental Health, United States, 1992.* Rockville, MD: U. S. Dept. of Health and Human Services.

Marans, S. and Cohen, D. (1993). Children and inner-city violence: Strategies for intervention. In L. Leavitt and N. Fox (Eds.), *Psychological Effects of War and Violence on Children.* Hillsdale, NJ: Erlbaum, pp. 281-302.

Marcus, R. F. (1991). The attachments of children in foster care. *Genetic, Social, and General Psychology Monographs, 117,* 365-194.

McCroskey, J., Nishimoto, R., and Subramanian, K. (1991). Assessment in family support programs: Initial reliability and validity testing of the Family Assessment Form. *Child Welfare, 70,* 19-33.

McGain, B. and McKinzey, R. K. (1995). The efficacy of group treatment in sexually abused girls. *Child Abuse and Neglect, 19,* 1157-1169.

Meichenbaum, D. (1977). *Cognitive-Behavior Modification: An Integrative Approach.* New York: Plenum Publishing Corp.

Mesmer, F. A. (1779). *Mémoire surla Decouverte de Magnetism Animal.* Paris: Didot.

Meyer, B. S. and Link, M. K. (1990). *Kinship Foster Care: The Double Edged Dilemma.* New York: Task Force on Permanency Planning for Foster Children.

Miller, D. (1993). Sexual and physical abuse among adolescents with behavioral disorders: Profiles and implications. *Behavioral Disorders, 18,* 129-138.

Montagu, A. (1968). Chromosomes and crime. *Psychology Today, 7,* 5, 43-49.

Moore, K. J. and Chamberlain, P. (1994). Treatment foster care: Toward development of community-based models for adolescents with severe emotional and behavioral disorders. *Journal of Emotional and Behavioral Disorders, 2,* 22-30.

Nissim, R. and Simm, M. (1994). Linking research and practice in fostering work—the art of the possible. *Adoption and Fostering, 18,* 10-17.

O'Connor, K. J. (1991). *The Play Therapy Primer: An Integration of Theories and Techniques.* New York: Wiley.

Ollindick, T. H. (1996). Socially aggressive and withdrawn children: Long-term outcomes. Paper presented at the Sixth Annual Virginia Beach Conference, Children and Adolescents with Emotional and Behavioral Disorders. Richmond, VA: October 4-8, 1996.

Osofsky, J. D. (1995). The effects of exposure to violence on young children. *American Psychologist, 50,* 782-788.

Patrick, M., Sheets, E., and Trickel, E. (1990). *We Are a Part of History: The Story of the Orphan Trains.* Santa Fe, NM: The Lightning Tree-Jene Lyon.

Patterson, G. R., Capaldi, D., and Bank, L. (1991). An early starter model for predicting delinquency. In D. I. Pepler and K. H. Rubin (Eds.), *The Development and Treatment of Childhood Aggression.* Hillsdale, NJ: Lawrence Erlbaum, pp. 139-168.

Patterson, G. R., Chamberlain, P., and Reid, J. B. (1982). A comparative evaluation of parent training procedures. *Behavior Therapy, 13,* 638-650.

Patterson, G. R., DeBaryshe, B. D., and Ramsey, E. (1989). A developmental perspective on antisocial behavior. *American Psychologist, 44,* 329-335.

Pelton, L. H. (1989). *For Reasons of Poverty: A Critical Analysis of the Public Child Welfare System in the United States.* New York: Praeger.

Pelton, L. H. (1991). Beyond permanency planning: Restructuring the public child welfare system. *Social Work, 36, 4,* 337-343.

Piaget, J. (1955). *The Moral Judgement of the Child.* New York: Macmillan.

Piaget, J. and Inhelder, B. (1956). *The Child's Conception of Space.* London: Routledge Kegan Paul.

Polsky, H. W. (1962). *Cottage Six: The Social System of Delinquent Boys in Residential Treatment.* New York: John Wiley and Sons.

Polsky, H. W. and Fast, J. (1993). Boot camps, juvenile offenders, and culture shock. *Child and Youth Care Forum, 22,* 403-415.

Price, W. H. and Whatmore, P. B. (1967). Criminal behavior in the XYY male. *Nature, 213,* 815-818.

Prilleltensky, I. (1997). Values, assumptions, and practices: Assessing the moral implications of psychological discourse and action. *American Psychologist, 52,* 517-535.

Pynoos, R. S. (1993). Traumatic stress and developmental psychopathology in children and adolescents. In J. M. Oldham, M. B. Riba, and A. Tasman (Eds.), *American Psychiatric Review of Psychiatry.* Volume 12. Washington, DC: American Psychiatric Press, pp. 205-239.

Pynoos, R. S. and Eth, S. (1985). Developmental perspectives on psychic trauma in childhood. In R. C. Figley (Ed.), *Trauma and Its Wake.* New York: Brunner/Mazel, pp. 36-52.

Quay, H. C. (1986). Classification. In H. C. Quay and J. S. Werry (Eds.), *Psychopathological Disorders of Childhood.* Third edition. New York: John Wiley and Sons, pp. 1-34.

Ray, J. and Horner, W. C. (1990). Correlates of effective therapeutic foster parenting. *Residential Treatment for Children and Youth, 74,* 57-69.

Ray, J., Smith, V., Peterson, T., Gray, J., Schaffner, J., and Houff, M. (1995). A treatment program for children with sexual behavior problems. *Children and Adolescent Social Work Journal, 12,* 331-343.

Reeder, R. R. (1909). *How Two Hundred Children Live and Learn.* New York: Charities Publication Committee. Reprinted (1974). New York: Arno Press.

Reid, J. B. and Patterson, G. R. (1989). The development of antisocial behavior in childhood and adolescence. *European Journal of Personality, 3,* 107-119.

Rice, D. M. and Rosen, M. (1991) The direct care worker: A neglected priority. *Mental Retardation, 29,* iii-iv.

Rice, D. M., Rosen, M., and Macmann, G. M. (1991). Attitudes of direct care workers at a residential facility. *Journal of Developmental and Physical Disabilities, 3,* 59-67.

Rosen, M. (1992). Service delivery in an institution: A case study. *McGill Journal of Education, 27,* 389-398.

Rosen, M. (1993). In search of the behavioral phenotype: A methodological note. *Mental Retardation, 31,* 177-178.

Rosen, M., Clark, G. R., and Kivitz, M. S. (1976). *The History of Mental Retardation: Collected Papers,* Volume 1. Baltimore, MD: University Park Press.

Rousseau, J. J. (1913). *The Social Contract and Discourses.* Trans. G. D. H. Cole. London: J. M. Dent, pp. 207-238.

Sabini, J. (1992). *Social Psychology.* New York: W. W. Norton.

Sagi, A. and Hoffman, M. L. (1976). Empathic distress in the newborn. *Developmental Psychology, 12,* 175-176.

Sarason, L. G. and Sarason, B. R. (1987). *Abnormal Psychology: The Problem of Abnormal Behavior.* Fifth edition. Englewood Cliffs, NJ: Prentice-Hall.

Satir, V. M. (1982). *Conjoint Family Therapy,* Third edition. Palo Alto, CA: Science and Behavior Books.

Schachter, S. and Singer, J. E. (1962). Cognitive, social and physiological determinants of emotional state. *Psychological Review, 69,* 379-399.

Scheerenberger, R. C. (1970). Generic services for the mentally retarded and their families. *Mental Retardation, 8,* 10-16.

Scheerenberger, R. C. (1982). Public residential services, 1981: Status and trends. *Mental Retardation, 20,* 210-215.

Scott, E. M. (1993). Prison group therapy with mentally and emotionally disturbed offenders. *International Journal of Offender Therapy and Comparative Criminology, 37,* 131-145.

Seguin, E. (1976a). Origin of treatment and training of idiots. In M. Rosen, G. R. Clark, and M. S. Kivitz (Eds.), *The History of Mental Retardation: Collected Papers.* Volume 1. Baltimore, MD: University Park Press, pp. 151-159. (Original work published 1864.)

Seguin, E. (1976b). Psycho-physiological training of an idiotic hand. In M. Rosen, G. R. Clark, and M. S. Kivitz (Eds.), *The History of Mental Retardation: Collected Papers.* Volume 1. Baltimore, MD: University Park Press, pp. 162-167. (Original work published 1879.)

Seguin, E. (1976c). Psycho-physiological training of an idiotic eye. In M. Rosen, G. R. Clark, and M. S. Kivitz (Eds.), *The History of Mental Retardation: Collected Papers.* Volume 1. Baltimore, MD: University Park Press, pp. 171-180. (Original work published 1880.)

Seligman, M. E. P. (1990). *Learned Optimism.* New York: Pocket Books.

Shapiro, S. H. (1973). Vicissitudes of adolescence. In S. L. Copel (Ed.), *Behavior Pathology of Childhood and Adolescence.* New York: Basic Books, pp. 93-117.

Shealy, C. N. (1995). From Boys Town to Oliver Twist. Separating fact from fiction in welfare reform and out-of-home placement of children and youth. *American Psychologist, 50,* 565-580.

Silbert, M. H. and Pines, A. M. (1981, July-August). Early sexual exploitation as an influence in prostitution. *Social Work,* 285-289.

Singh, N. N., Epstein, M. H., Luebke, J., and Singh, Y. N. (1990). Psychopharmacological intervention. I: Teacher perceptions of psychotropic medication of students with serious emotional disturbance. *The Journal of Special Education, 24,* 283-295.

Skeels, H. M. and Dye, H. B. (1939). A study of the effects of differential stimulation of mentally retarded children. *Proceedings and Addresses of the American Association on Mental Deficiency, 44,* 114-136.

Slater, M. A. and Bunyard, P. D. (1983). Survey of residential staff roles, responsibilities, and perception of resident needs. *Mental Retardation, 21*, 52-58.

Smith, J. D. (1985). *Minds Made Feeble: The Myth and Legacy of the Kallikaks.* Rockville, MD: Aspen Press.

Sovner, R. and Weisblatt, S. (1992). The significance of psychotic symptoms in diagnosis and treatment. Paper presented at the First International Congress on the Dually Diagnosed. Boston, MA: April 30, 1992.

Spurzheim, J. G. (1834). *Phrenology.* Boston: Marsh, Coper, and Lyon.

Steele, B. F. and Alexander, H. (1981). Long-term effects of sexual abuse in childhood. In P. B. Mrazek and C. H. Kempe (Eds.), *Sexually Abused Children and Their Families.* New York: Pergamon, pp. 223-233.

Stennis, W. (1973). Ego disturbances in children. In S. L. Copel (Ed.), *Behavior Pathology of Childhood and Adolescence.* New York: Basic Books, pp. 60-92.

Stilwell, B. M., Galvin, M., Kopta, S. M., and Padgett, R. J. (1996). Moral valuation: A third domain of conscience functioning. *Journal of the American Academy of Child and Adolescent Psychiatry, 35*, 230-239.

Stone, M. H. (1974). Mesmer and his followers: The beginnings of sympathetic treatment of childhood emotional disorders. *Journal of Psychohistory, 1*, 659-679.

Strauss, A. and Lehtinen, L. (1947). *Psychopathology and Education of the Brain-Injured Child.* New York: Grune and Stratton.

Stroul, R. A. and Friedman, R. M. (1986). *A System of Care for Severely Emotionally Disturbed Children and Youth.* Washington, DC: XASSP Technical Assistance Center, Georgetown University Child Development Center.

Tatara, T. (1992). *Characteristics of Children in Substitute and Adoptive Care—Based on FY82 Through FY88 Data.* Washington, DC: American Public Welfare Association.

Teicher, M. H., Clod, C., and Cole, J. O. (1990). Emergence of intense suicidal preoccupation during Fluoxetine treatment. *American Journal of Psychiatry, 142*, 2, 207-210.

Thaw, J. and Wolfe, S. F. (1986). The direct-care workers: A sociocultural analysis. In J. Thaw and A. Cuvo (Eds.), *Developing Responsive Human Services: New Perspectives about Residential Treatment Organizations.* Hillsdale, NJ: Lawrence Erlbaum, pp. 83-147.

Thompson, R. W., Authier, K., and Ruma, P. (1994). Behavior problems of sexually abused children: A preliminary study. *Journal of Child Sexual Abuse, 3*, 79-91.

Trieschman, A. E. (1976, Summer). The Walker School: An education-based model. *Child Care Quarterly, 5*, 123-135.

Trieschman, A. E., Whittaker, J., and Brendtro, L. (1969). *The Other 23 Hours.* Chicago: Aldine.

Tushman, M. L. and O'Reilly, C. A., III. (1997). *Winning Through Innovation: A Practical Guide to Leading Organizational Change and Renewal.* Boston: Harvard Business School Press.

U.S. Department of Health and Human Services. (1992). R. W. Manderescheid and M. A. Sonnenschein (Eds.), *Mental Health, United States, 1992.* Rockville, MD: U.S. Government Printing Office.

Vanbiema, D. (1994). The storm over orphans. *Time, 144,* 24, December 12, 58-62.

Walker, C. E., Bonner, B. L., and Kaufman, K. L. (1988). *The Physically and Sexually Abused Child.* New York: Pergamon.

Walton, M. (1986). *The Deming Management Method.* New York: Putnam.

Watson, J. B. (1924). *Behaviorism.* New York: Norton.

Weisblatt, S. (1994). Diagnosis of psychiatric disorders in persons with mental retardation. In N. Bouras (Ed.), *Mental Health in Mental Retardation.* New York: Cambridge University Press.

White, J., Carrington, J., and Freeman, P. (1990). *A Study of the Educational Status of Foster Children in Oregon: Research and Statistics.* Portland: Oregon Department of Human Resources, Children's Services Division.

Whitney, E. A. and Shick, M. McD. (1976). Some results of selective sterilization. In M. Rosen, G. R. Clark, and M. S. Kivitz (Eds.), *The History of Mental Retardation: Collected Papers.* Volume 2. Baltimore, MD: University Park Press, pp. 201-210. (Original work published 1931.)

Wilson, J. E. and Sherrets, S. D. (1979). A review of past and current pharmacological intervention in the treatment of emotionally disturbed children and adolescents. *Behavioral Disorders, 5,* 60-69.

Witmer, L. (1896). The organization of practical work in psychology. *Proceedings of the Fifth Annual Meeting of the American Psychological Association, 4,* 116-117.

Wolfensberger, W. (1971a). Will there always be an institution? I: The impact of epidemiological trends. *Mental Retardation, 9,* 14-20.

Wolfensberger, W. (1971b). Will there always be an institution? II: The impact of new service models. *Mental Retardation, 9,* 31-38.

Wollons, R. (1993). *Children at Risk in America: History, Concepts and Public Policy.* Albany: State University of New York Press.

Yacoubian, J. H. and Lourie, R. S. (1973). Suicide and attempted suicide in children and adolescents. In S. L. Copel (Ed.), *Behavior Pathology of Childhood and Adolescence.* New York: Basic Books, pp. 149-165.

Zahn-Waxler, C., Radke-Yarrow, M., and King, R. A. (1979). Child rearing and children's prosocial inclinations toward victims of distress. *Child Development, 50,* 319-330.

Zeanah, C. H. (1994). The assessment and treatment of infants and toddlers exposed to violence. In J. D. Osofsky and E. Fenechel (Eds.), *Caring for Infants and Toddlers in Violent Environments: Hurt, Healing and Hope.* Arlington, VA: Zero to Three/National Center for Clinical Infant Programs, pp. 29-37.

Zigler, E. and Hodapp, R. M. (1986). *Understanding Mental Retardation.* New York: Cambridge University Press.

Zlomke, L. C. and Benjamin, V. A., Jr. (1983). Staff inservice: Measuring effectiveness through client behavior change. *Education and Training of the Mentally Retarded, 18,* 125-130.

# Index

# *Order Your Own Copy of*
# *This Important Book for Your Personal Library!*

## TREATING CHILDREN IN OUT-OF-HOME PLACEMENTS

_____ in hardbound at $39.95 (ISBN: 0-7890-0163-2)

_____ in softbound at $24.95 (ISBN: 0-7890-0893-9)

COST OF BOOKS_____

OUTSIDE USA/CANADA/
MEXICO: ADD 20%_____

POSTAGE & HANDLING_____
*(US: $3.00 for first book & $1.25*
*for each additional book)*
*Outside US: $4.75 for first book*
*& $1.75 for each additional book)*

SUBTOTAL_____

IN CANADA: ADD 7% GST_____

STATE TAX_____
*(NY, OH & MN residents, please*
*add appropriate local sales tax)*

**FINAL TOTAL**_____
*(If paying in Canadian funds,*
*convert using the current*
*exchange rate. UNESCO*
*coupons welcome.)*

☐ **BILL ME LATER:** ($5 service charge will be added)
(Bill-me option is good on US/Canada/Mexico orders only;
not good to jobbers, wholesalers, or subscription agencies.)

☐ Check here if billing address is different from
shipping address and attach purchase order and
billing address information.

Signature_____

☐ **PAYMENT ENCLOSED: $**_____

☐ **PLEASE CHARGE TO MY CREDIT CARD.**

☐ Visa   ☐ MasterCard   ☐ AmEx   ☐ Discover
☐ Diner's Club
Account #_____

Exp. Date_____

Signature_____

Prices in US dollars and subject to change without notice.

NAME_____

INSTITUTION_____

ADDRESS_____

CITY_____

STATE/ZIP_____

COUNTRY_____ COUNTY (NY residents only)_____

TEL_____ FAX_____

E-MAIL_____
May we use your e-mail address for confirmations and other types of information? ☐ Yes   ☐ No

*Order From Your Local Bookstore or Directly From*
**The Haworth Press, Inc.**
10 Alice Street, Binghamton, New York 13904-1580 • USA
TELEPHONE: 1-800-HAWORTH (1-800-429-6784) / Outside US/Canada: (607) 722-5857
FAX: 1-800-895-0582 / Outside US/Canada: (607) 772-6362
E-mail: getinfo@haworthpressinc.com
PLEASE PHOTOCOPY THIS FORM FOR YOUR PERSONAL USE.

BOF96